Spiritual Florida

Spiritual FLORIDA

A GUIDE TO
Retreat Centers
AND
Religious Sites
IN FLORIDA AND NEARBY

Mauricio Herreros

PINEAPPLE PRESS, INC.
SARASOTA, FLORIDA

The purpose of this book is to be a practical guide about the diverse spiritual places and unique religious sites in Florida and surrounding areas. This is not a book about the different religious faiths practiced in Florida and surrounding areas. The author and the publisher respect all religions and it is not the objective of this book to try to convert anyone to a particular denomination.

Inquiries should be addressed to:
Pineapple Press, Inc.
P.O. Box 3889
Sarasota, Florida 34230
www.pineapplepress.com

Photos: Private collection of the author

Library of Congress Cataloging in Publication Data
Herreros, Mauricio.
    Spiritual Florida : a guide to retreat centers and religious sites in Florida and nearby / Mauricio Herreros.-- 1st ed.
      p. cm.
    Includes bibliographical references and index.
    ISBN 1-56164-331-9 (pbk : alk. paper)
    1. Spiritual retreat centers--Florida--Directories. 2. Monasteries--Guest accommodations--Florida--Directories. 3. Spiritual retreat centers--Southern states --Directories. 4. Monasteries--Guest accommodations--Southern States-- Directories. I. Title.
      BL2527.F6H47 2005
      206'.5'025759--dc22
                    2005002221

First Edition
10 9 8 7 6 5 4 3 2 1

Design by ospreydesign, www.ospreydesign.com
Printed in the United States of America

To

Lorrie, Sara, Christian and Jonathan . . .
and to all those on the spiritual path
that you may find the Way . . .

Also by

MAURICIO HERREROS:

*Simply Running: An Inspirational and
Common Sense Guide to Running*

*Running in Florida: A Practical Guide for
Runners in the Sunshine State*

Contents

Acknowledgments

I want to thank my wife Lorrie for her invaluable support in this endeavor. She reviewed each section numerous times, always with a smile. I am especially thankful to my wonderful kids for their love and kindness, allowing me to spend hundreds of hours working on this book and not with them.

Many thanks to all the nice people I met during my visits to spiritual centers throughout Florida and the Southeast who provided me with the insight for this project.

Special thanks to the following individuals who went out of their way to answer my questions: Father Joseph from Panagia Vlahernon Monastery; Than Chaokhun Phra Vijitrdhammapani, head monk at the Wat Florida Dhammaram; and Sister Mary from the Monastery of Saint Clare. Many thanks to Sister Kathleen from Marywood Retreat Center for her encouragement and to Brother Michael from Holy Spirit Monastery for his spiritual inspiration and friendship.

Many thanks always to my parents, Humberto and Patricia, for a lifetime of love and trust.

June and David Cussen, my supportive publishers, and the staff at Pineapple Press, thank you for your work in making this undertaking a reality.

Introduction

Have you ever wondered what it would be like to go on a spiritual retreat? Have you heard others talk about the physical, mental, and spiritual benefits they received in these experiences? Do you sometimes feel like you need a break from the demands and pressures of daily life? Well, spending a weekend, a few days, or even just an hour away from the world may be exactly what you need and perhaps unknowingly have been looking for.

The reality is that people have been going on retreats and spiritual pilgrimages for centuries. In the old days people visited monasteries and journeyed to sacred shrines. In our time people continue to go to monasteries and religious sites, but now there are many more options. Today more than ever before retreats are open to all, not just the clergy or religious orders.

Florida and its neighboring states have a significant number of monasteries, spiritual retreat centers, and unique religious sites that offer a place where you can be in a peaceful, secluded, and spiritually nurturing setting. *Spiritual Florida* is a complete guide to such places for the Sunshine State and the nearby Southeast. The book includes detailed descriptions of each spiritual place with information about its history, facilities, retreat programs, contacts, and directions.

Traveling through Florida, Georgia, South Carolina, and parts of Alabama, I found a rich and alive spirituality that extends subtly across cultures and religious denominations. The book that you hold in your hands reflects the diverse spectrum of spiritual options found in the

Southeast. It is the result of thousands of miles of driving and hundreds of hours of research. *Spiritual Florida* features over fifty spiritual places, each unique and ready to be discovered. *Spiritual Florida* can be a valuable companion on your spiritual journey.

How to Use
This Book

For easy reference, *Spiritual Florida* has been divided into four
major sections:

North Florida
Central Florida
South Florida
Beyond Florida

The first three sections correspond to the three main geographical
regions of the state of Florida. The fourth section, Beyond Florida, is
for places outside Florida but located within a day's drive. This section
covers the states of Alabama, Georgia, and South Carolina.

The featured places are listed in alphabetical order regardless of their
geographical location within the region or their denomination. To find
a place by location within a region, check the map and legend on the
next two pages. To find a place by type of religion, consult the index.
With a few exceptions, for each place the information provided includes
a description of the location, a brief history, the religious denomination,
the type of facilities available, the range of programs offered, directions
to the site, and contact information.

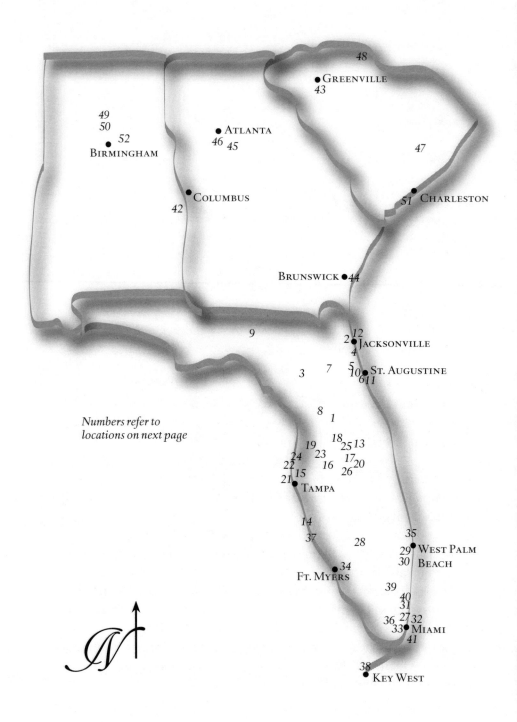

48

● GREENVILLE
43

49
50
 52
● BIRMINGHAM

● ATLANTA
46 45

47

● COLUMBUS
42

● CHARLESTON
51

BRUNSWICK ● 44

9

2 12
4 ● JACKSONVILLE

3   7   5
          10 ● ST. AUGUSTINE
          6 11

8   1

19   18 25 13
24 23   17
22 16   20
15   26
21 ● TAMPA

14
37   28   35
                    29 ● WEST PALM
                    30   BEACH

34   39
● FT. MYERS   40
              31
36 27 32
33 ● MIAMI
41

38
● KEY WEST

*Numbers refer to
locations on next page*

The places in this book were chosen because of their spiritual uniqueness, their openness, and the types of programs available. When deciding which places to include, the following guidelines were considered:

-Is it a retreat center, monastery, unique shrine, or
　sacred religious site?
-Is it well established, in existence at least five years?
-Is it nonprofit?
-Is it open to the public?
-Is it open to retreats?
-Is it open to all denominations?
-Is it spiritual?

The Resources section provides a list of websites with additional spiritual places as well as a list of general spirituality references. A list of bibliographic references is included at the end of the book.

The purpose of *Spiritual Florida* is twofold: to put together in one book all the unique and diverse spiritual places in Florida and surrounding areas, and to offer an easy-to-use guide to the thousands of people looking for a spiritual place in the Sunshine State and beyond. Though every effort has been made to provide up-to-date and accurate information, some changes may take place from time to time, so it is advisable to call ahead before making a journey.

I am interested in hearing from readers as they explore their own spiritual paths. Have you discovered a special place that could be included in a future edition? If so, please contact me at Pineapple Press, P.O. Box 3889, Sarasota, FL 34239.

Going on Retreat

According to *The American Heritage Dictionary* a retreat is "a period of seclusion, retirement, or solitude." A retreat is a time away from the pressures of ordinary life in a quiet and peaceful place. The length of a retreat is variable. It can be a few hours, a day, a weekend, or longer. A spiritual retreat setting should provide an atmosphere that encourages reflection, silence, meditation, and prayer.

Going on a spiritual retreat can be a truly refreshing experience. In fact, many people feel transformed after such an event. Perhaps it is the sense of peace and harmony found, or the special sacredness of spiritual places. In reality, no words can clearly describe these experiences for you; you must find out for yourself by going to these places.

If you have never been on a spiritual retreat before, you may have a few questions about types of retreats, costs, what to expect, meals, and proper etiquette. Below are some guidelines to help you get the best out of these unique experiences.

TYPES OF RETREATS

The most common types of spiritual retreats are group and individual retreats. Although some retreats can last a day or less, most require an overnight stay.

Group Retreats: These retreats combine spiritual talks in a group setting with time on your own for reflection, meditation, and prayer. Although some group retreats are specially scheduled for a private institution, most are open to anyone as long as there is room available.

Individual Retreats: These retreats are usually divided into directed and private retreats. The main difference between these two is that directed retreats include meeting with a spiritual director during your stay. In private retreats you are on your own.

Costs

In general the costs per retreat are relatively low, but vary depending on length and type of retreat. Many places are run by nonprofit religious institutions that have a suggested donation per day. Others have a set fee per retreat. In most instances, these centers are self-sustaining and rely on these fees to help them cover their operating expenses.

What to Expect

Whether it is a monastery or a more open retreat center, you can expect to find a place of peace and tranquility. Most spiritual places are secluded and surrounded by beautiful grounds that are conducive to reflection and spiritual nourishment. Expect a positive and uplifting experience. Depending on the place and the type of retreat, you may have more or less time on your own. Monasteries generally encourage guests to participate in the daily prayer services with the monks or nuns. This alone can be an unforgettable experience.

Meals

The retreat food is usually home-cooked style and healthy. Most places provide meals in their retreats unless expressed otherwise. When in doubt ask the retreat center in advance of your visit.

Proper Etiquette

The rules of etiquette are very similar throughout all spiritual places. Below are some tips to keep in mind when visiting these beautiful places:

- Casual dress is usually okay but many places, especially monasteries, do not allow shorts, tank-tops, mini-skirts, or revealing clothes. The idea is to dress conservatively with respect for the spiritual setting.

- Most retreat centers provide linen and towels, but ask ahead of time to make sure. Usually the only things you need to bring are your personal hygiene items and clothes.
- It is said that in silence we hear the voice of God. Many retreat centers provide an environment that fosters silence. It is important to respect the guidelines of each place and help maintain a quiet atmosphere. Often there are designated areas for silence and for talking. In some monasteries meals are eaten in silence.
- One of the purposes of retreats is to be away from the distractions of the world. For this reason many retreat centers do not provide a phone, TV, or radio in the bedrooms. This is a very valuable aspect of the retreat experience.
- If you bring a cell phone make sure to keep it in silent mode and use it only in designated areas.
- While on retreat you will likely come across other retreatants. Each person is there for his or her own reasons. Some people are there to experience solitude, not to engage in conversation.

When planning a spiritual retreat it is important to allow plenty of advance time since overnight space is limited and scheduled retreats fill up quickly. The more flexibility you have, the easier it will be to find the desired dates or scheduled retreat event.

Spiritual Places in
North Florida

ANNUNCIATION OF THE
THEOTOKOS MONASTERY
Reddick

nnunciation of the Theotokos is a Greek Orthodox monastery for women located off Highway 225 in Reddick (Marion
County). The Annunciation of Theotokos Monastery was established
in 1998 by a group of nuns under the auspices of the Greek Orthodox
Archdiocese of America. The sisters trace their spiritual roots to the
Holy Monastery of Saint John the Forerunner in Serres, Greece. This
historic thirteenth-century monastery became a convent in 1986 and is
a very popular pilgrimage site.

Annunciation of the Theotokos Monastery, Reddick

The Annunciation of Theotokos Monastery is situated in an area of much natural charm with green fields and horse farms nearby. The monastery church and buildings are set far away from the main entrance. Follow the signs along the peaceful road to the monastery. The guesthouse is located on the right about halfway between the entrance and the monastery. The grounds are well kept with flowers and many trees. The monastery building is at the end of the paved road. The icons in the small chapel are very beautiful. There is a bookstore that sells religious articles, music, books, and high quality incense made by the sisters.

The Greek word Theotokos means "Mother of God," and the monastery is dedicated to her. Every year in March the Annunciation of Theotokos feast is celebrated at the monastery. Many monks and nuns from other monasteries, as well as lay people, come to this event. The nuns follow a strict schedule of daily prayers, liturgy, and services. Overnight stays are available but are limited to women. These must be prearranged. The monastery is open daily to visitors.

When visiting the monastery proper attire is required. Women should wear a head scarf and a dress that covers the knees; no shorts, mini-skirts, or low-necked blouses are permitted. Men should wear long-sleeved shirts and long pants; no shorts or T-shirts are allowed. When in doubt, ask the nuns.

DIRECTIONS AND INFORMATION

Annunciation of the Theotokos Monastery's address is 13486 N.W. Highway 225, Reddick, Florida 32686. The monastery is located a few miles west of I-75, between Gainesville and Ocala. The entrance is on the north side of Highway 225.

For information call (352) 591-1803 or visit their website www. holyannunciation.org. The website offers information in both English and Greek.

2

BETHEL BAPTIST INSTITUTIONAL CHURCH
Jacksonville

*L*ocated in downtown Jacksonville, Bethel Baptist Institutional Church is a unique church with a rich history. Listed in the National Register of Historic Places, Bethel Baptist Institutional Church is not only one of the largest African-American churches in the state of Florida but is one of the oldest. The congregation first organized in 1838 as Bethel Baptist Church. The present-day church building is Florida's oldest existing Baptist church. It was completed in 1904 after the original church burned down in the Great Fire of 1901, which destroyed most of Jacksonville. Bethel Baptist Institutional Church is a vibrant

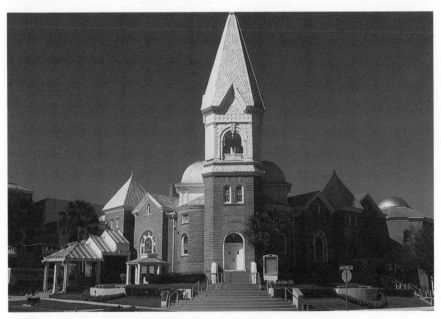

Historic Bethel Baptist Institutional Church in Jacksonville

4

place. In fact, for many decades it has been the center of religious and community activities for African-Americans in northeast Florida.

The church's architecture is beautiful, with a neoclassical style that stands out for its simple lines and varied roof types. The church complex occupies an entire city block; its buildings include the educational center, administration offices, and the impressive sanctuary and family life center. There are also several classrooms, a library, cafeteria, and an archives museum. The church museum maintains a valuable collection of historic documents and artifacts.

In addition to regular church services, Bethel Baptist Institutional Church offers many other events, including Bible study groups, revival retreats, women's programs, men's programs, as well as youth and children's programs.

Bethel Baptist Institutional Church is open to people of all denominations.

DIRECTIONS AND INFORMATION

Bethel Baptist Institutional Church's address is 215 Bethel Baptist Street, Jacksonville, Florida 32202. The church is 1 block north of State Street and 1 block west of Laura Street, across from the Florida Community College (FCCJ) downtown campus.

For information or to schedule a tour of the church and archives museum, call (904) 354-1464 or visit their website www.bethelite.org.

3

CAMP KULAQUA
RETREAT CENTER
High Springs

*C*amp Kulaqua is a popular retreat center located in High Springs, just south of the Santa Fe River. Camp Kulaqua opened in 1953 and, with its seven hundred acres of pristine property, is one of the largest Seventh-day Adventist retreat centers in the world. Initially the center was primarily established as a youth summer camp, but over the years it expanded into a dynamic Christian retreat center for all.

The extensive retreat center has many buildings and outdoor facilities. The beautiful grounds encompass a natural spring, many live oaks, grassy areas, walking paths, picnic areas, and lots of shade. For overnight

Leaving Camp Kulaqua Retreat Center in High Springs

stays the retreat center offers several types of air-conditioned housing options, including guest rooms, cabins, family chalets, and mini-lodges. An RV site is also available. The center maintains a large cafeteria with various meal alternatives for guests. There is also a general store that sells Christian books, snacks, and a wide range of souvenirs. Camp Kulaqua has three chapels available for events and meetings. In addition, the camp has several outdoor recreation facilities, including a private zoo and nature center, amphitheater, and its very own water park.

Camp Kulaqua hosts many scheduled programs throughout the year, including women's retreats, men's retreats, singles' retreats, and family camps. Because it provides a safe and peaceful atmosphere, the center attracts many people to its retreats and events, including families, church groups, youth groups, and individuals seeking a quiet and restful place.

For the latest schedules and retreat information, contact the center directly or check their website. Camp Kulaqua is open to all denominations.

DIRECTIONS AND INFORMATION

Camp Kulaqua's address is 700 N.W. Cheeota Avenue, High Springs, Florida 32643. Cheeota Avenue (N.W. 212th Avenue) runs off US 441 about 1.5 miles north of High Springs and before crossing the Santa Fe River. The camp gate is at the end of Cheeota Avenue, just under a mile from US 441. Camp Kulaqua is located west of I-75.

For information call (386) 454-1351 or visit their website www. campkulaqua.com.

4

FIRST BAPTIST CHURCH
Jacksonville

Known as the miracle of downtown Jacksonville, First Baptist Church is a very impressive place. Originally organized in 1838, the church underwent many changes before it settled at its present location in 1892. Since then First Baptist Church has continued to grow steadily over the years. Today the church campus extends across nine city blocks, making it one of the largest churches in the country. Some of the church buildings include a large worship center that seats ten thousand, a welcome center, a library, a bookstore, multiple educational facilities, auditoriums, and several indoor parking garages.

First Baptist Church is a popular and active Christian center. First-time visitors are encouraged to attend the guest reception following the Sunday morning worship service in order to learn more about the church, its history, and the opportunities available. In addition to the worship services, the church offers many programs year-round, including Bible classes and events for seniors, families, singles, men, women, and children. First Baptist Church has a beautiful retreat center located on the St. Marys River, just west of Hilliard along the Florida-Georgia border. The retreat facility has cabins and is used for overnight church retreats and youth camps.

For schedule information on services and events, contact the church directly or check their website. First Baptist Church is open to people of all denominations.

DIRECTIONS AND INFORMATION
First Baptist Church's address is 124 W. Ashley Street, Jacksonville, Florida 32202. The welcome center is on Ashley Street, just west of

Main Street. The worship center is 1 block north, at the intersection of Beaver and Laura Streets.

For information call (904) 356-6077 or visit their website www. fbcjax.com.

*First Baptist Church
in downtown Jacksonville*

5

MARYWOOD RETREAT CENTER
Switzerland

*M*arywood Retreat Center is a tranquil retreat complex nestled on over one hundred acres of native woodlands along the St. Johns River in northeast Florida. Located just south of Jacksonville, in the northwest corner of St. Johns County, Marywood is operated by the Catholic Diocese of St. Augustine. The center started offering retreats in 1979, but it was in 1989 when the newer buildings were completed that Marywood took its present shape.

The Marywood entrance is visible from State Road 13 right past (if you are going south) the San Juan del Rio Catholic Church. The paved road winds through secluded woods for over a half mile to the banks of the river where the Marywood buildings and chapel are located. This buffer of nature between the main road and the river is perhaps what makes one quickly feel a world apart. Parking is available at the end of the entrance road under the live oaks. From this point, straight ahead you see the big Spanish-style stone house or "Casa." This was built in 1938 as a private residence and today it is home to the beautiful Marywood Chapel and the main administrative offices. Right across from the Casa is the Kelly Center, where the reception desk, library, conference room, bookstore, and dining room are located. The dining room serves buffet-style meals for guests daily; the food is very good. The bookstore/gift shop offers a variety of books, music, and religious items. Outside, between the Kelly Center and the river there is an open grassy area with a stone prayer labyrinth. The prayer labyrinth derives from an ancient tradition in medieval Europe, where Christian pilgrims used to walk the labyrinth as a symbol of their spiritual journey. Many cathedrals built prayer labyrinths for this purpose.

The Marywood Chapel is unique and a must-see for visitors. Inside the chapel one feels a sacred presence, the all-encompassing peace of the place. Sitting alone in the chapel one late summer afternoon, I felt humbled by the view through the windows. For a moment time seemed to stop with the reflection of the sun's rays on the calm waters flowing unceasingly past the giant live oaks on the river's edge. Outside the chapel a path leads to the long wide wooden dock that reaches out several hundred feet into the magnificent St. Johns River. This is definitely worth the walk. The view is spectacular.

Marywood offers many overnight retreats throughout the year. Three fully air-conditioned buildings with motel-style rooms, each with its own private bathroom, stand to the left of the Kelly Center. The rooms are very comfortable with double and single beds. In addition Marywood has several other facilities, including meeting rooms, a large swimming pool and picnic area, tennis courts, and a dormitory-style building geared to group camps, which is located on the north end of the property. A scenic nature trail with the Stations of the Cross along

*Marywood Retreat Center on the
St. Johns River, Switzerland*

the way is located across from the Casa. Ask the Marywood staff for directions. The trail is wooded and almost three quarters of a mile long.

One noticeable thing about the Marywood grounds is that everything is within walking distance, yet there is ample space for finding solitude. Silence prevails. Marywood is truly a spiritual place, a sort of hidden gem waiting to be discovered. Many who have come here return again and again to this special place on the banks of the St. Johns River.

Marywood Retreat Center is open year-round to people from all denominations. Scheduled retreats are offered regularly. Private retreats are available as well. Many people attend day seminars and group events. Others just come to visit for a few hours. Most scheduled group retreats are held on weekends. If looking for a private retreat usually there is room available during the week, but call ahead to confirm. Overnight stays require a fee per night to cover room and board expenses. Most seminars have a set fee, although some simply ask for a donation. Always check specific details with the Marywood staff. For scheduled retreats and seminars check the website or call the center directly.

DIRECTIONS AND INFORMATION

Marywood Retreat Center's address is 1714-5 State Road 13, Jacksonville, Florida 32259. The entrance to Marywood is located behind the San Juan del Rio Catholic Church, off State Road 13 in Switzerland.

For information call (904) 287-2525 or visit their website www.marywoodcenter.org.

6

Memorial Presbyterian Church
St. Augustine

*M*emorial Presbyterian Church is a unique place in Florida. Located within a block of Flagler College in St. Augustine, this beautiful church was built in 1889 by Henry Flagler in memory of his daughter Jennie Louise Benedict. The church architecture is Venetian Renaissance–style and was modeled after the Saint Mark's Cathedral in Venice. Inside, the church is filled with rich detail and beauty. Henry Flagler spared no expense in the construction of the building. He sought out the finest materials and hired the best architects, sculptors and workers of the time. Italian marble was brought for the floors and

The historic Memorial Presbyterian Church in St. Augustine

Italian artists decorated the huge copper dome. The woodwork is hand-carved Santo Domingo mahogany and the baptismal font was crafted of a solid piece of Sienna marble. The stained-glass windows designed by a German artist took twelve years to complete and were made by the Decorative Glass Company of New York.

A mausoleum was built adjacent to the church (near the entrance to the left). This is accessible through a short hallway. Henry Flagler, his wife, daughter, and granddaughter are buried here.

Outside one can easily appreciate the architectural splendor of this church with its impressive dome, many intricate details, and peaceful gardens. It is said that Henry Flagler wanted this church to stand out above all other churches in St. Augustine. He certainly succeeded.

Memorial Presbyterian Church is open daily to the public.

Directions and Information

Memorial Presbyterian Church's address is 32 Sevilla Street, St. Augustine, Florida 32084. The church is located at the intersection of Sevilla and Valencia Streets.

For services and general information call (904) 829-6451 or visit their website www.memorialpcusa.org.

7

MONTGOMERY CONFERENCE CENTER
Starke

*M*ontgomery Conference Center is a peaceful retreat center located halfway between Keystone Heights and Starke in northeast Florida. The center is a ministry of the Presbyterian Church and is operated by the Presbytery of St. Augustine.

Montgomery Center is spread out over a large beautiful wooded area with pristine lakes. The grounds are very natural with majestic live oaks, pine trees, and secluded nature trails. The center has a dining hall, several conference rooms, covered pavilions, and a rustic outdoor chapel overlooking Crystal Lake. The overnight facilities include equipped

The Williams Lodge at Montgomery Conference Center, Starke

cabins, a lodge with dormitory-style accommodations, and several motel-style private rooms with bathrooms. In addition the center offers plenty of outdoor amenities such as canoeing, a challenge course, a high ropes course, a swimming lake area, and a playground.

Montgomery Center hosts many scheduled retreats, workshops, and conferences throughout the year. Church groups, youth groups, companies, and families are just some of the people who visit this center. Some events are overnight and some are just for the day, but regardless of the length of stay all that come benefit from the serene setting of Montgomery.

For retreat information and available schedule contact the center directly or check their website. Montgomery Conference Center is open to all denominations.

Directions and Information

Montgomery Conference Center's address is 88 S.E. 75th Street, Starke, Florida 32091. The entrance road to the Montgomery Center is located off County Road 18, about 30 yards from the intersection with State Road 100.

For information call (352) 473-4516 or visit their website www.montgomerycenter.org.

8

PANAGIA VLAHERNON
MONASTERY
Williston

*P*anagia Vlahernon is a Greek Orthodox monastery located on 140 acres off Highway 318 in Levy County, just south of Gainesville and north of Ocala. The monastery was founded in early 1999 by a group of monks from the Saint Anthony Monastery in Arizona, which in turn had come from the monastery of Philotheou on Mount Athos in Greece. The small monastic community came to Florida with the mission of bringing the pure tradition and uncompromised teachings of the Holy Orthodox Faith to the faithful.

Main entrance to Panagia
Vlahernon Monastery, Williston

Panagia Vlahernon Monastery is dedicated to the Mother of God and was named after the famous fifth-century Church of Panagia of Blachernae (Vlahernes) in Constantinople (present-day Istanbul). The original church is now destroyed, but several miracles were attributed to it, including the Deposition of the robe of the Most Holy Mother of God. This is when the robe of Mary was brought from Nazareth in the fifth century and placed in the Church of Panagia of Blachernae. This event is commemorated at Panagia Vlahernon Monastery every July. Other important Orthodox feasts are celebrated throughout the year at the monastery. The monks live a simple life dedicated to prayer, work, and service. In the Orthodox monastic tradition daily liturgies and vesper services are very important, as are fasting, confession, and communion.

The first thing that caught my attention when I arrived at the Panagia Vlahernon Monastery was the sight of two monks working outside in the midday summer heat. Dressed in a black tunic and wearing a straw hat, one of them approached. Father Joseph greeted me and went out of his way to make me feel at home. Although I explained to him that I

The monastery church at Panagia Vlahernon

am not an Orthodox Christian, he showed me around and spent almost two hours describing the Orthodox monastic life and answering my questions. He was most friendly and invited me to return for a longer visit. Talking with Father Joseph helped me realize how valuable monasteries are in keeping alive the spirituality of the faith.

The area surrounding the monastery is very rural, with gentle slopes and farms. The monastery church and buildings are not visible from the outside road. As you turn into the main entrance you will pass the monastery sign. The narrow road winds around for about a quarter of a mile before you see the monastic buildings. There is a pond on the left and a big two-story house ahead. This is the monks' residence. The church and other buildings are located further up past the house. The grounds are very picturesque with live oaks, benches, and open meadows giving a welcoming parklike atmosphere. The monastery church is small but very beautiful with a great aura of peace, a true spiritual treasure. Next to the church are the refectory (dining area) and the bookstore. The bookstore has a large selection of religious icons, articles, and books in both Greek and English. The overnight guesthouse is situated to the right of the church. It has a small living room, bathroom with shower, and several single beds. It is air-conditioned and comfortable. There is no TV. There is no fee for overnight stays, which include room and board. Donations are accepted but not required. Overnight retreats are primarily for men and families. Because space is limited, pre-arrangements are required. Contact the monastery with plenty of advance time if interested in staying overnight.

During services in the monastery church, men sit on the right side and women sit on the left side of the church. When visiting the monastery you are asked to adhere to the dress code. All guests should be modestly dressed. Men should wear long-sleeved shirts and long pants, no shorts or T-shirts. Women should wear a head scarf and a dress that covers the knees, no shorts, mini-skirts, or low-necked blouses. Ask the monks when in doubt.

Panagia Vlahernon Monastery is open daily for visits.

DIRECTIONS AND INFORMATION

Panagia Vlahernon Monastery's address is 12600 W. Highway 318, Williston, Florida 32696. The monastery is located on Highway 318 about 5 miles west of the I-75 exit. The entrance is on the south side of Highway 318.

For information call (352) 591-1716 or visit their website www.panagiavlahernon.org. The website offers information in both English and Greek.

9

SAINT JOHN NEUMANN RENEWAL CENTER
Tallahassee

he Saint John Neumann Renewal Center is a well-established spiritual retreat center located in Tallahassee. The Roman Catholic center started in the early 1980s and it is operated under the direction of the Diocese of Pensacola-Tallahassee. One of the retreat center's main objectives is to provide spiritual help to all those who attend the various workshops and seminars held at the center. Over the years many people have come to this place.

The facility was a Catholic convent of nuns prior to becoming a retreat center. The overnight accommodations are simple but comfortable. The center has a beautiful chapel. Saint John Neumann Renewal Center offers scheduled spiritual retreats, workshops, and weekly classes throughout the year. Private retreats are also possible depending on availability. A suggested fee is required for most events to help cover expenses.

For specific information on available retreats and upcoming seminars contact the center directly. Saint John Neumann Renewal Center is open to people of all denominations.

DIRECTIONS AND INFORMATION

The Saint John Neumann Spiritual Renewal Center's address is 685 Miccosukee Road, Tallahassee, Florida 32308. The retreat center is situated near the intersection of Washington Street, a few blocks north of Tennessee Street (US 90).

For retreat information call (850) 224-2971.

10

SAINT PHOTIOS GREEK ORTHODOX
NATIONAL SHRINE
St. Augustine

The Saint Photios Greek Orthodox National Shrine is an institution of the Greek Orthodox Archdiocese of America. Located in the center of historic St. Augustine, this sacred and unique site is also known as "the jewel of St. George Street."

Saint Photios Shrine opened in February 1982 as a living memorial dedicated to the first Greek settlers that came to America in 1768 arriving in the area of New Smyrna in Florida. The shrine is named in honor of Saint Photios the Great, who was Patriarch of Constantinople during the middle of the ninth century and greatly admired as

St. Photios National Shrine, St. George Street, St. Augustine

theologian, defender of the faith, and supporter of missionary activity. The mission of the shrine is not only to honor the first colony of Greek immigrants, but also to preserve, enhance, and promote the ethnic and cultural traditions of Greek heritage and the teachings of the Greek Orthodox Church in America. A traditional pilgrimage to the Saint Photios Greek Orthodox National Shrine is held every year in early February to celebrate the feast of Saint Photios the Great, the shrine's patron saint. All are welcome to attend this weekend event.

At the Saint Photios Shrine you will find a small museum with several exhibits of artifacts, photographs, and historical documents describing the life and struggles of the first Greek pioneers in Florida. The beautiful Saint Photios Chapel is located here as well. As you enter this holy place you will see an area with candles on the right and left. This is where you can make an offering by lighting a candle. The first things that you will notice are the walls of the chapel, which are filled with magnificent Byzantine-style frescoes of scenes from the early Christian Church. The central dome depicts Christ the Pantocrator (the All-Embracing) and the four Evangelists. The rich color and detail of the paintings can cause one to stand in awe contemplating their beauty and meaning. The inscriptions on the paintings are in Greek. Brochures are available describing the chapel frescoes and their religious significance.

Outside the chapel in addition to the pioneer exhibit there are other special displays, including a unique relic box given by the Vatican to the Greek Orthodox Church of America. The box is said to contain very tiny fragments of bone from several of the apostles, including Saint Peter and Saint Paul. There is a small gift shop/bookstore where you can get books, music, icons, and other traditional Greek products. This is a good place to find more information about the shrine.

Saint Photios Shrine is perhaps a little hidden in the middle of the bustling noise and distractions of popular St. George Street. Many people walk by every day unaware of the spiritual peace found behind the plain white walls, but for those who do notice and venture inside, the discovery can be spiritually rich, maybe even life-changing.

DIRECTIONS AND INFORMATION

The Saint Photios Greek Orthodox National Shrine's mailing address is P.O. Box 1960, St. Augustine, Florida 32085. The physical address is 41 St. George Street in downtown St. Augustine. The Shrine is open daily. Call for specific hours. There is no admission fee but donations are welcomed.

For general information call (904) 829-8205 or visit their website www.stphotios.com.

11

SHRINE OF OUR LADY
OF LA LECHE
St. Augustine

The Shrine of Our Lady of La Leche is located within the tranquil grounds of the Mission of Nombre de Dios along the Matanzas Bay waters in St. Augustine. The historic Mission of Nombre de Dios is America's first mission dating back to the founding of St. Augustine in 1565. It is here that on September 8, 1565, Pedro Menéndez de Avilés landed and knelt to kiss a wooden cross presented to him by Father Francisco López de Mendoza Grajales, the chaplain of the expedition. It was on this sacred site that the first parish Mass in the nation was celebrated, and it was here that the long and arduous Christian missionary work began in the United States.

The original Shrine of Our Lady of La Leche Chapel was built around 1615 by Spanish settlers and was dedicated to the Blessed Virgin Mary. The chapel was dismantled and abandoned in the early part of the eighteenth century during an attack on St. Augustine. The shrine was rebuilt in 1873 and was subsequently destroyed by a hurricane a year later. The present-day shrine was built in 1915 and it contains a replica of the original statue of Nuestra Señora de la Leche y Buen Parto (Our Lady of the Milk and Happy Delivery). Over the decades the shrine has become a special place of prayer for expectant mothers and for all those seeking quiet reflection. In the year 2000, Pope John Paul II designated the Shrine of Our Lady of La Leche as a place of pilgrimage for all.

The architecture of the shrine is of Spanish mission–style. Inside, the small chapel is simple with wooden benches and an altar for Mass. Offering candles are found along the sides by the entrance. The famous statue of Mary nursing the infant Jesus is visible behind the altar. Outside the chapel, the grounds are very beautiful and peaceful with live oaks and cedar trees, and numerous gravestones, some of which date back to the 1800s. There are several historic memorials, including a rustic altar commemorating the site of the first Mass located near the water, a bell tower, and statues of Saint Francis of Assisi and Saint Joseph found by the chapel. A large 208-foot tall steel cross is located by the waterfront. The Great Cross was erected as a memorial of the four hundredth anniversary of the mission. The view of the Matanzas Bay from the grounds is lovely. A gift shop with a wide selection of books, statues, church supplies, and religious articles is near the main entrance to the mission. Restrooms and a water fountain are available in the gift shop.

St. Francis at the Shrine of Our Lady of La Leche, St. Augustine

The mission and shrine are open daily. Admission is free, but donations are welcomed. These help with costs of maintaining the grounds and memorials. There is ample free parking available.

Both the Mission of Nombre de Dios and the Shrine of Our Lady of La Leche are not only unique spiritual places, they are an important part of this nation's history of peoples and cultures across the centuries.

Shrine of Our Lady
of La Leche, St. Augustine

DIRECTIONS AND INFORMATION
The Mission of Nombre de Dios and the Shrine of Our Lady of La Leche's address is 27 Ocean Avenue, St. Augustine, Florida 32084. Ocean Avenue is off San Marco Avenue, just north of Castillo Drive.

For more information call (904) 824-2809 or visit their website www.missionandshrine.org.

*The 208-feet tall Great Cross at the
Shrine of Our Lady of La Leche in St. Augustine*

12

WAT KHMER SAVY RATTANARAM
Jacksonville

Secluded in a quiet middle-class residential neighborhood in Jacksonville, the Wat Khmer Savy Rattanaram is one the most important Cambodian Buddhist temples in the country. Although the present-day temple was completed in late 2004, the project began in 1996 when Cambodian refugees donated the three-acre property to establish an authentic holy site for the growing Cambodian community in the area. The architecture of the temple was inspired by traditional Buddhist religious sites in Southeast Asia. Wat Khmer Savy Rattanaram was built following the strictest Buddhist rules, such as the one requiring

Wat Khmer Savy Rattanaram, Jacksonville

that twenty-eight columns support the exterior of the temple. The intricate carving designs on the windows and doors are replicas from Angkor Wat, the world-famous twelfth-century temple in northwestern Cambodia. The large Buddha inside the temple and all the stone statues outside were brought from Cambodia as well.

Wat Khmer Savy Rattanaram is a welcoming place. The surrounding grounds are pleasing and peaceful. Several Buddhist monks live at the site. They are very friendly. Wat Khmer Savy Rattanaram has regular weekend services and celebrates the traditional Buddhist holidays. There is a community center available too. If you visit, keep in mind that it is the Buddhist custom to take off your shoes before entering the temple. Wat Khmer Savy Rattanaram is open daily. All people are welcome.

DIRECTIONS AND INFORMATION

Wat Khmer Savy Rattanaram's address is 4540 Clinton Avenue, Jacksonville, Florida 32207. The temple is at the intersection of Clinton and Turner Avenues, about 0.3 miles east of Philips Highway. Clinton Avenue is 1.1 miles north of University Boulevard.

For information call (904) 739-5896.

Spiritual Places in
Central Florida

13

CANTERBURY RETREAT AND CONFERENCE CENTER
Oviedo

*T*he Canterbury Retreat and Conference Center is a scenic retreat center nestled on more than forty acres of pristine woodland on Lake Gem in Oviedo. The center opened in the early 1980s and is a ministry of the Episcopal Diocese of Central Florida. The center's mission is to offer a sanctuary of hospitality for growth and learning, a place "where the beauty of God's creation invites rest and relaxation."

The retreat center facilities include comfortable air-conditioned motel-style rooms with private bathrooms. The rooms have no phones or TVs in order to minimize outside distractions. The center has several lounges, meeting rooms, and a lakeside dining hall. A beautiful chapel and a smaller oratory are open for meditation and services. A bookstore with a large selection of books, music, and religious items is available as well. Outside, the well-tended grounds are very peaceful with many trees, lush vegetation, and secluded paths. The area's natural atmosphere is conducive for quiet reflection and spiritual introspection.

Canterbury Retreat and Conference Center offers various types of retreats and scheduled programs year-round. Retreats are available for individuals, couples, families, and groups. For specific retreat information and event schedules contact the center directly or check their website. Canterbury Retreat and Conference Center is open to people of all denominations.

DIRECTIONS AND INFORMATION

Canterbury Retreat and Conference Center's address is 1601 Alafaya Trail (State Road 434), Oviedo, Florida 32765. The retreat center is a few miles north of the University of Central Florida campus. Oviedo is northeast of Orlando.

For information call (407) 365-5571 or visit their website www.canterburyretreat.org.

14

CHRISTIAN RETREAT
Bradenton

*C*hristian Retreat is a large and vibrant interdenominational retreat center situated on more than one hundred acres along the banks of the scenic Manatee River in Bradenton. Christian Retreat has been operating for many years, attracting people from all faiths who come to this center for spiritual conferences, church events, and family retreats.

As you turn off Upper Manatee River Road onto Glory Way Boulevard, you will see a community of homes on both sides of the street. The retreat center is located past the homes straight ahead. Christian

Main entrance to the Christian Retreat in Bradenton

Retreat has several buildings. The registration office is to the right of the entrance in the Miracle Manor building. From the registration lobby there is a great view of the lagoon and landscaped grounds below. The center has plenty of comfortable air-conditioned motel-style rooms. An RV campground is also available. The center has a large dining facility that serves buffet-style meals daily. A small bookstore/gift shop is located inside the Tabernacle auditorium building. In addition there are many recreational amenities, including an Olympic-size swimming pool, tennis courts, basketball courts, picnic areas, and a playground. The grounds are very peaceful with live oaks, palm trees, and colorful flowers. The natural beauty of the area invites visitors to reflection and prayer.

Christian Retreat hosts a variety of scheduled events year-round, including national conferences, youth events, Bible study programs, and group retreats. There are women's retreats, men's retreats, singles' retreats, couples' getaways, and church retreats. Individual retreats are available as well. The center's atmosphere is friendly and family-oriented.

Christian Retreat is open to individuals and groups of all denominations.

DIRECTIONS AND INFORMATION

Christian Retreat's address is 1200 Glory Way Boulevard, Bradenton, Florida 34212. Glory Way Boulevard is located off Upper Manatee River Road (a few miles east of I-75).

For information call (941) 746-2882 or visit their website www.christianretreat.org.

15

FRANCISCAN
CENTER
Tampa

The Franciscan Center is a beautiful and popular Roman Catholic retreat place located on the banks of the Hillsborough River in Central Tampa. The center is staffed by volunteers and by the Franciscan Sisters of Allegany, New York. The Franciscan Center opened in 1970 and was originally the home of a Tampa attorney who donated the eight-acre riverfront property for religious and educational purposes.

Over the years the Franciscan Center has become a spiritual sanctuary on the west coast of Florida. Thousands of people visit the center every

Franciscan Center, Tampa

year to attend seminars, workshops, and retreats. Following the tradition of Saint Francis of Assisi, the Franciscan Center is dedicated to offering a nurturing environment of peace, simplicity, and hospitality.

The center's two-story main building has a dining room, library, conference area, and a chapel. The single and double private bedrooms are air-conditioned and have bathrooms with showers. Bed linens and towels are provided. The meals are prepared by the staff and are very good. There is a small gift store that sells books, music, and other Franciscan items. A separate retreat house near the main center is available for small groups or individuals.

The surrounding grounds are very welcoming with big live oak trees, ample green lawns, and the spectacular view of the river. Several benches and chairs are available throughout so visitors can rest and relax for a while. The area's natural beauty is conducive to prayer, reflection and spiritual enrichment. There is sense of divine tranquility and peace.

The Franciscan Center is open to all. There are several types of retreats available, including private retreats, guided retreats (with a spiritual director), and special group retreats. Retreats can vary in length from a weekend to a week or longer. There is a fee per day for each type of retreat. To schedule a retreat or to find out available dates it is best to call well in advance since space is limited. In addition to the overnight retreats, the Franciscan Center hosts many community day workshops and events throughout the year. To find out more about these check their website or contact the center directly.

DIRECTIONS AND INFORMATION
The Franciscan Center's address is 3010 N. Perry Avenue, Tampa, Florida 33603. From Martin Luther King Jr. Boulevard take N. Ridge Avenue (this is on the east side of the Hillsborough River). Continue on Ridge Avenue. Turn right on Fribley Street and then left on Perry Avenue. The center is ahead on the right side (between Adalee Street and Braddock Street).

For information call (813) 229-2695 or visit their website www. fsalleg.org.

16

HOLY NAME MONASTERY
St. Leo

*T*he Holy Name Monastery is a Roman Catholic Benedictine monastery founded in 1889 by five sisters from Saint Joseph Convent in Pennsylvania who came to Florida with the mission to establish a Catholic academy for children. The sisters operated a boarding academy and a boy's preparatory school in the San Antonio and St. Leo area for many years. Although the number of sisters has varied over time, the Benedictine Sisters of Florida have successfully continued the educational tradition of service to schools, to the community, and to God. As followers of the Rule of Saint Benedict, the sisters seek to lead

Holy Name Monastery, St. Leo

a balanced monastic life of prayer, work, community, solitude, contemplation, and active ministry.

The present-day monastery building was built in the 1960s and is located along scenic Lake Jovita at the west end of the campus of Saint Leo Abbey and Saint Leo University. Holy Name Monastery is a center for spiritual direction, Christian teaching, ministry programs, prayer, contemplation, and Benedictine values.

Holy Name Monastery offers spiritual retreats for women and men of all faiths. Some of the retreat types include private individual retreats, directed retreats with the guidance of a spiritual director, scheduled vocation retreats for women discerning a call to religious life, and special group retreats (these must be prearranged). Sabbatical experiences are also possible for women who wish to spend some time living in a monastic community while pursuing their own program of interest, including prayer, relaxation, leisure, and solitude. Additionally, a Benedictine live-in volunteer program is available for women that meet a few specific requirements.

If you are considering a spiritual retreat, the beautiful Holy Name Monastery grounds provide a natural setting and serene atmosphere conducive to spiritual reflection and renewal. To schedule a private retreat or to find out available dates call the monastery well in advance since space is limited. The private guest rooms are air-conditioned and linens are provided. Common bathrooms are located in the monastery building. Guests can share meals with the sisters and are invited to attend the Eucharist and Liturgy of the Hours. The monastery chapel is always open. A suggested donation fee per day is expected to help cover the expenses of room and board.

DIRECTIONS AND INFORMATION

Holy Name Monastery's mailing address is P.O. Box 2450, St. Leo, Florida 33574. The physical address is 33201 State Road 52, just under 4 miles east of I-75, and within walking distance (quarter of a mile) from Saint Leo Abbey and Saint Leo University.

For general information call (352) 588-8320 or visit their website www.floridabenedictines.com.

17

Islamic Society of
Central Florida
Orlando

*E*stablished in the 1970s, the Islamic Society of Central Florida is a nonprofit religious organization dedicated to serving the diverse growing Muslim community of greater Orlando. The organization oversees several mosques (masajids) and schools in the area. The Islamic Society of Central Florida operates a center that offers weekly prayers, social services, and religious classes. Additionally, the center actively works to convey the message of Islam to the non-Muslim community in central Florida through exhibits at the Dawah Center, special events, and educational programs.

Although most activities at the Islamic Society of Central Florida are intended for Muslims, some are open to people of other faiths. For hours, event schedules, or questions, contact the center directly or check their website.

Directions and Information
The Islamic Society of Central Florida's mailing address is P.O. Box 338, Goldenrod, Florida 32733. The center's physical address is 1089 N. Goldenrod Road, Orlando, FL 32807.

For information call (407) 273-8363 or visit their website www.iscf. org.

18

LAKE YALE BAPTIST CONFERENCE CENTER
Leesburg

The Lake Yale Baptist Conference Center is a large and active retreat facility located along Lake Yale in the Leesburg area. The center opened in the 1960s and is operated by the Florida Baptist Convention, an organization of Baptist churches and associations. Covering more than 280 acres, the wooded grounds provide a very tranquil atmosphere with live oaks, walking trails, colorful gardens, and the scenic lake. The area's natural setting is conducive to quiet reflection and intimacy with God's beautiful creation.

Lake Yale Baptist Conference Center has a number of buildings with comfortable motel-style accommodations. The center has a big auditorium, various conference rooms, a lakeside dining room, a bookstore, and lounge areas. There are two youth camp areas with air-conditioned dormitory-style cabins, separate cafeterias, and chapels. In addition, there are several outdoor facilities, including a swimming pool, an amphitheater, recreation fields, and an RV park.

Lake Yale Baptist Conference Center offers retreats, youth camps, and events year-round. Overnight retreats are available for groups of various sizes, churches, and families. For retreat information and program schedules, contact the center directly or check their website. Lake Yale Baptist Conference Center is open to people of all denominations.

The Florida Baptist Convention also operates a smaller retreat facility (Blue Springs Baptist Conference Center) in Marianna in the Florida Panhandle area.

DIRECTIONS AND INFORMATION

The Lake Yale Baptist Conference Center's address is 39034 County Road 452, Leesburg, Florida 34788. The center is about 48 miles northwest of Orlando and only a few miles north of Eustis.

For information call (800) 226-8584 or (352) 483-9800 or visit their website www.flbaptist.org.

19

LAKEWOOD
RETREAT
Brooksville

*L*akewood Retreat is a picturesque Christian retreat center located in the Brooksville area. The retreat facility is operated by the Southern Mennonite Camping Association. The family-oriented center is situated on over one hundred acres of scenic woodlands along Hancock Lake, providing a rustic and peaceful atmosphere. Lakewood Retreat has a number of lodging facilities, including cabins, mini-lodges, motel-style rooms, and campsites. The center has meeting rooms, a dining hall, and a lovely outdoor chapel by the lake. Some of the outdoor amenities include nature trails, recreational fields, tennis courts, a tree house, a swimming pool, and canoes.

Lakewood Retreat offers several scheduled group retreats, youth camps, and programs year-round. Retreats are available for groups, churches, and families. Day visitors are welcome. For retreat information and schedules, contact the center directly or check their website. Lakewood Retreat is open to people of all denominations.

DIRECTIONS AND INFORMATION

The Lakewood Retreat center's address is 25458 Dan Brown Hill Road, Brooksville, Florida 34602. The center is north of Tampa.

For information call (352) 796-4097 or visit their website www.lakewoodretreat.org.

20

MARY, QUEEN OF THE UNIVERSE SHRINE
Orlando

*M*ary, Queen of the Universe Shrine is an impressive Roman Catholic Church located on a twenty-two-acre complex in the vicinity of the Lake Buena Vista area in Orlando. The Shrine stands as an oasis of tranquility amidst the busy tourist attractions nearby. Mary, Queen of the Universe is an institution of the Diocese of Orlando and it was declared a house of pilgrimage by Pope John Paul II.

The original Shrine Church opened in April 1986 as a place dedicated to serving the spiritual needs of the large numbers of tourists visiting the area. With the passing of time the shrine has continued to grow. Construction of the present-day Marian Church started in 1990 and was completed in January 1993. Inside, the spacious 2000-seat Shrine Church has high ceilings and a long line of white arched columns on each side. The church is adorned with fourteen inspirational stained-glass windows and above the circular altar is a striking 650-pound portrayal of the crucified Christ. The Blessed Sacrament Chapel (Perpetual Adoration) is located around the back of the church (to the right of the main altar) through the doors. The Chapel of Our Lady of Guadalupe is on the left side by the front of the church. Outside, across the courtyard to the right is the Mother and Child Chapel with a prominent eighty-foot tower. This outdoor chapel has a unique twelve-foot bronze sculpture of the Mother and Child created by noted artist Jerzy Kenar.

There is a big gift shop in the building across the courtyard to the left. Many religious items are available here, including rosaries, books, and statues. A small shrine museum with paintings, sculptures, and historic church art is located next to the gift shop.

Beautiful outdoor chapel at Mary, Queen of the Universe Shrine, Orlando

The impressive Mary, Queen of the Universe Shrine, Orlando

The shrine's well-maintained surrounding grounds are very peaceful with walkways, colorful flowers, trees, ponds, and fountains. A beautiful Rosary Garden with a statue of Mary holding the Child Jesus is located outside beyond the gift shop building along the left side of the church.

Mary, Queen of the Universe Shrine is open to all people. The Shrine Church is open daily from 7:30 a.m. to 5:00 p.m. For Mass schedule, museum and gift shop hours, call the shrine directly or check the website.

DIRECTIONS AND INFORMATION

Mary, Queen of the Universe Shrine's address is 8300 Vineland Avenue, Orlando, Florida 32821. Vineland Avenue runs off State Road 535, just south of the I-4 exit (Lake Buena Vista exit). Vineland Avenue goes parallel to I-4. Mary, Queen of the Universe Shrine is located in the area of Little Lake Bryan. Follow the signs to Mary Queen Shrine.

For information call (407) 239-6600 or visit their website www.maryqueenoftheuniverse.org.

21

OUR LADY OF
DIVINE PROVIDENCE
Clearwater

*O*ur Lady of Divine Providence House of Prayer is a quiet retreat center nestled on the banks of the Old Tampa Bay in Clearwater. The retreat center opened in 1980 and it is a ministry of the Marian Servants of Divine Providence, a private association of the Roman Catholic faith.

The retreat complex sits on a waterfront area of about fifteen acres which includes several buildings and retreat houses. Each house is unique and fully equipped for overnight retreats with private bedrooms and bathrooms. A chapel is available for prayer and quiet reflection.

One of several retreat houses, Our Lady of Divine Providence, Clearwater

Mass is offered here. The center maintains a library with many spiritual books and tapes. Outside, there is a beautiful rose garden with a Pieta statue surrounded by a walkway with the Stations of the Cross. The grounds are peaceful with big live oaks, green lawns, delicate gardens, benches, and paths. Also, the view of the bay is breathtaking.

Our Lady of Divine Providence offers several types of retreats year-round, including scheduled weekend retreats, private retreats, and Ignatian retreats. Private retreats can include spiritual direction (directed) or no spiritual direction (nondirected). Ignatian retreats are more intense and last longer. They are based on the spiritual exercises of Saint Ignatius of Loyola, and include daily spiritual direction, reading of the scriptures, prayer, and meditation. In addition, the center offers study programs on various spiritual topics.

There is a suggested donation for overnight retreats to help cover the expenses of room and board. Because availability is limited, contact the retreat center with plenty of advance time. For the latest retreat schedule, call the center directly or check their website. Our Lady of Divine Providence House of Prayer is open to all.

DIRECTIONS AND INFORMATION

Our Lady of Divine Providence's address is 725 S. Bayview Avenue, Clearwater, Florida 33759. S. Bayview Avenue is a street off Gulf-To-Bay Boulevard (Highway 60) about a quarter of a mile west of the Bayside Bridge/ McMullen-Booth Road intersection (Highway 611). The retreat center is located on the south side about a block from Gulf-To-Bay Boulevard.

For information call (727) 799-4003 or visit their website www. divineprovidence.org.

22

PARBAWATIYA BUDDHIST CENTER
Safety Harbor

*P*arbawatiya Buddhist Center opened in 1996 and it was the first center of Kadampa Buddhism to be established in Florida. Parbawatiya Center is a member of the New Kadampa Tradition (NKT). This is an international association of hundreds of Buddhist centers around the world. The New Kadampa Tradition was started by the contemporary Buddhist master Geshe Kelsang Gyatso, and it derives its guidance from the teachings and example of ancient Kadampa Buddhist masters. Kadampa Buddhism is a specific tradition of the Mahayana Buddhism denomination and was founded by the Indian Buddhist Master Atisha in the eleventh century. It is said that Atisha was responsible for the reintroduction of Buddhism into Tibet. The followers of Atisha are known as Kadampas. Kadampa Buddhism offers Buddha's teachings in a way that is easy to understand and to apply to daily life. For this reason many Kadampa Buddhism teachers and practicioners are Westerners.

Parbawatiya Center occupies a beautiful corner house on a peaceful street near the historic center of Safety Harbor. The center offers meditation retreats, ongoing study programs, seminars, and meditation classes for various levels of experience, including beginners.

Parbawatiya Center is open to all. The center is nonprofit. A small suggested fee may apply for classes and other events. During workdays most classes are held in the evening. For hours and event schedules, call the center or check their website.

In addition to the Parbawatiya Center there are several other Kadampa Buddhist meditation centers in Florida. For locations and specific information check the website.

DIRECTIONS AND INFORMATION

Parbawatiya Center's address is 201 6th Avenue S. , Safety Harbor, Florida 34695. The center is located at the intersection of 6th Avenue S. and 2nd Street S. , 1 block south of Main Street in downtown Safety Harbor. Safety Harbor is just east of Clearwater on the Old Tampa Bay side, and a couple of miles north of the Courtney Campbell Causeway (Highway 60).

For information call (727) 797-9770 or visit their website www.meditationinflorida.org.

The Parbawatiya Buddhist Center
in beautiful Safety Harbor

23

SAINT LEO ABBEY
St. Leo

Saint Leo Abbey is a Roman Catholic Benedictine monastery founded in 1889 by a group of monks from Saint Vincent's Archabbey in Pennsylvania. The Abbey was named after Pope Leo XIII, Pope Saint Leo the Great, and Abbot Leo Haid of Saint Mary Help Abbey in North Carolina, who accepted the responsibility for the emerging Saint Leo community.

Located amid the beautiful rolling hills and orange groves of Pasco County in central Florida, Saint Leo Abbey is an oasis of Christian spirituality, tranquility, and monastic hospitality. Following the Rule of Saint Benedict, the monks of Saint Leo Abbey live a simple life dedicated to seeking God through daily prayer, solitude, humility, and work.

Saint Leo Abbey, Saint Leo University, and Holy Name Monastery are all within walking distance of each other. Together these institutions have passed the Benedictine tradition from generation to generation and continue today to be the beacon of Benedictine values in Florida.

Saint Leo Abbey is located off State Road 52 in the town of St. Leo. The abbey is a little hidden from the road because there is no direct entrance. To get to the abbey area you have to go through Saint Leo University's main entrance and turn left on the service road and continue for a few hundred yards. Then you will see the abbey's sign on your right. Another option is to park in the university parking lot left of the entrance and walk towards the Abbey Church. There is a path that leads to the front of the church.

The beautiful church and bell tower were completed in 1948. Their architecture is of Lombardic-Romanesque style. Inside the church there is a large marble crucifix over the main altar, which was modeled after the imprinted image of Christ on the Shroud of Turin. It is believed that this carving is the largest copy of the shroud ever produced. The monastery building is behind the Abbey Church, and the retreat house is the building to the right of the church. The abbey's welcome center is located in a small house to the left of the front of the church, across from the gift shop. The welcome center has information and brochures. The abbey's gift shop is a great place to find books, monastery products, and other religious items.

St. Leo Abbey Church,
St. Leo

The abbey's natural grounds are very welcoming with scenic walking paths and many varieties of trees, including live oaks, cedars, cypresses, and palm trees. Rows of orange trees are seen along the beautiful Lake Jovita, which is accessible behind the monastery building. The abbey's grotto is located across State Road 52 and west of the Saint Leo Abbey Golf Course. There are posted signs, but ask for directions if you are unsure. The grotto was built many years ago by one of the resident

Side view of the church at
St. Leo Abbey, St. Leo

monks as a pilgrimage site for prayer. It is very peaceful and spiritually inspiring. Here you will find a cave in honor of Our Lady of Lourdes, and a statue of the Risen Christ. The abbey's first Abbot, Charles Mohr, is buried here, and there is a shrine to the Saint Leo schoolboys who died during World War II.

Saint Leo Abbey offers spiritual retreats throughout the year. These are open to men and women of all faiths. Married couples can be accommodated as well. The types of retreats include private retreats, private directed retreats (spiritual guidance provided), weekend retreats, special group retreats (must be prearranged), and scheduled youth retreats. If staying overnight is not an option the abbey offers prescheduled group day retreats, which include a meal and talks with the monks or lay staff. If you just want to visit, Saint Leo Abbey is open daily and self-guided walking tours are encouraged. Men considering the monastic life are invited to contact the abbey's vocational director.

The multi-story retreat house is very comfortable. The private rooms have a bed, desk, lamp, chair, and an air-conditioning window unit. There are no distractions such as phone, radio, or TV. Some rooms have a private bathroom but most don't. There are bathrooms and showers on each floor. Bed sheets and towels are provided. You need to bring only your personal items. When I stayed at Saint Leo Abbey my room had a view of the monastery building and the lake behind. It was very quiet and serene. The abbey's meals are home-cooked and self-service style. The food is very good and healthy. Retreatants eat their meals with the monks, which I truly enjoyed during my weekend visit. Retreat guests are invited to participate in the daily prayers with the monks. Five times per day the monks gather in the Abbey Church to worship God. A suggested donation fee per day is required to help cover the cost of meals and room.

Whether seeking a special place for a spiritual retreat or simply looking for a peaceful refuge from a busy lifestyle, Saint Leo Abbey offers an ideal environment for body rest and soul nourishment. Retreat space is limited so contact the Abbey's retreat center with plenty of advance time.

DIRECTIONS AND INFORMATION

Saint Leo Abbey's mailing address is P.O. Box 2350, St. Leo, Florida 33574. The physical address is 33601 State Road 52, St. Leo, Florida 33574. The abbey is about 4 miles east of I-75. Saint Leo Abbey is adjacent to Saint Leo University. To get to the Abbey area, go through the main university entrance and turn left. Saint Leo Abbey is located about 30 miles north of Tampa.

For general information call (352) 588-8624. For retreat questions, including schedules, call the retreat center at (352) 588-8182. For all of the above visit their website www.saintleoabbey.org.

24

SAINT NICHOLAS GREEK ORTHODOX CATHEDRAL
Tarpon Springs

*L*ocated in historic Tarpon Springs on the Gulf of Mexico, the Saint Nicholas Greek Orthodox Cathedral is an institution of the Greek Orthodox Archdiocese of America. Tarpon Springs, also known as the sponge-diving capital of the world, is a lively west Florida seaside town with a strong Greek influence going back to the beginning of the twentieth century. This is when many Greek immigrants from the Dodecanese Islands started to arrive attracted by the thriving sponge industry. Today this charming community offers the feel of an authentic Greek village with many restaurants, bakeries, boutiques, and fishing boats along the sponge dock area.

The first Saint Nicholas Greek Orthodox Church in Tarpon Springs was built in 1907. Over time with the continuous growth of the Greek community it became necessary to build a new church. The present-day Saint Nicholas Greek Orthodox Cathedral was completed in 1943. The new church is of Neo-Byzantine architecture and was designed as a replica of the famous Saint Sophia Cathedral in Constantinople (now Istanbul). All the marble in the church was brought from Greece.

Inside the church there is much detail to admire with traditional Greek Orthodox icons, colorful stained-glass windows, a beautiful dome, arches, unique carvings, lamps, and candles. The Weeping Icon of Saint Nicholas is found near the entrance. Saint Nicholas is the patron saint of the sponge fishing community in Tarpon Springs. It is said that in early December 1970 a woman cleaning the church noticed tears around the eyes of the icon. In the following days and years many more people saw the tears coming from the eyes of the Saint Nicholas icon. This usually occurred during the Christmas season and no explanation was ever found especially since the icon was tightly enclosed in a glass frame. Over the years, thousands of people of all faiths have made the pilgrimage to see the Weeping Icon of Saint Nicholas.

One of the most important sacred days in the Greek Orthodox tradition is the Epiphany. This day-long celebration is held on January 6th to commemorate the baptism of Jesus in the River Jordan when the Holy Spirit descended upon him in the form of a dove. Tarpon Springs is well-known for this event and thousands of visitors arrive every year for this celebration. During this day the schools close and families attend a morning liturgy at the Saint Nicholas Cathedral. After the service a procession walks to the nearby Spring Bayou, where the archbishop blesses the waters and casts a white wooden cross into the bayou. A young woman releases a dove, and a group of local boys, between the ages of sixteen through eighteen, plunge into the cold bayou waters in search of the Epiphany Cross. The belief is that retrieving the cross will ensure a year of good luck and blessing. Following the dive for the cross, the Epiphany events include traditional Greek foods, music, and dancing. It is believed that the Epiphany observance in Tarpon Springs surpasses the fame of all others, including similar events in Greece.

St. Nicholas Greek Orthodox Cathedral, Tarpon Springs

DIRECTIONS AND INFORMATION

The Saint Nicholas Greek Orthodox Cathedral's address is 36 N. Pinellas Avenue, Tarpon Springs, Florida 34689. The church is about a block north of Tarpon Avenue in downtown Tarpon Springs. Tarpon Springs is located off US 19, about 12 miles north of Clearwater. There is no admission fee to the church, but donations are welcomed.

For general information, call (727) 937-3540 or visit their website www.epiphanycity.org.

25

SAN PEDRO
CENTER
Winter Park

San Pedro Center is a picturesque and serene retreat center situated on over 450 acres along Lake Howell in Seminole County. Located only a few miles northeast of Orlando, San Pedro Center is a ministry of the Roman Catholic Diocese of Orlando. The center is staffed by a group of Franciscan Friars Third Order Regular (TOR), who are known for their hospitality and love of nature.

The Franciscan Friars lead a simple life of poverty, prayer, contemplation, chastity, obedience, and communal living in the spirit of their founder and patron, Saint Francis of Assisi. The friars are active in

San Pedro Center, Winter Park

retreat work, education, and in the larger community, providing spiritual enrichment, healing, and the sharing of the message of conversion in God's name.

In 1979 the first friars arrived at San Pedro Center. Over the years the center has become a much sought out place, a base for spiritual transformation in central Florida attracting thousands of people every year to attend workshops, seminars, and retreats.

At San Pedro Center one can't help but notice a marked feeling of tranquility. The green surroundings, the lush woods, the quiet walking trails, the lovely lake are all natural manifestations conducive to a spiritual peacefulness. San Pedro Center has a unique prayer labyrinth which is almost an exact replica of the labyrinth at the famous Chartres Cathedral in France. The prayer labyrinth derives from an ancient religious tradition which says that by walking the labyrinth's winding path that takes us to the center we symbolize our own spiritual journey. Many Gothic cathedrals in medieval Europe used labyrinths as substitutes for the pilgrimage to Jerusalem. The San Pedro Center prayer labyrinth is

The prayer labyrinth at San Pedro Center

definitely a landmark to experience during your visit. Look for it next to the friars' house.

San Pedro Center has a very beautiful chapel that invites visitors in for a moment of prayer and reflection. The center's overnight accommodations are very comfortable with several air-conditioned motel-like double rooms with private bathrooms. There is also a large dormitory-style facility with separate air-conditioned dormitories for men and women. Each dorm area has bathrooms. Bed linens and towels are provided. Additionally there are a few rustic lakeside cabins available for private retreats. The center has a large dining facility with home-cooked style meals that are very healthy and tasty. There is a small reading library room near the dining area and a bookstore. The bookstore has a varied selection of books, religious articles, and pottery art.

San Pedro Center offers workshops, seminars, and overnight retreats throughout the year. All people are welcome. In addition to private retreats and scheduled group retreats, there are several other types of events held. Some of these include young adult retreats, summer camps for youth, art studio programs, a spiritual direction formation program, Secular Franciscans meetings, and many community day seminars. For retreat information, event schedules, and fees, check the website or call the center directly.

DIRECTIONS AND INFORMATION

San Pedro Center's address is 2400 Dike Road, Winter Park, Florida 32792. Dike Road runs off Howell Branch Road in Casselberry (Seminole County). San Pedro Center is located on Lake Howell, just a few miles northeast of downtown Winter Park. San Pedro Center is open to people from all denominations.

For information call (407) 671-6322 or visit their website www. sanpedrocenter.org.

26

WAT FLORIDA DHAMMARAM
Kissimmee

The Wat Florida Dhammaram is a Buddhist monastery located just a few hundred yards from the busy tourist corridor of highway US 192 in Kissimmee. This religious sanctuary was founded in 1993 by a group of Thai monks from the Wat Sommanut Vihara monastery in Bangkok, Thailand. The monks came to central Florida with the mission to share the teachings of the Theravada Buddhist tradition, the strictest of the three main Buddhist branches. The word Wat means "temple" and Dhammaram translates to "school of doctrine."

Spread out over several acres, the Wat Florida Dhammaram monastery consists of a number of unique buildings. Some of these include the beautiful main temple (Uposoth), a school for the study of Dhamma (doctrine), the monks' residence house, a multipurpose hall, a Thai Teak House, and a traditional Thai-style bell tower. In addition there are four replicas of the famous Buddhist pilgrimage sites in India: The Siri Maha-Mayadevi Vihara of Lumbini which commemorates the Buddha's birth, the Mahabodhi Temple of Bodgaya which commemorates his enlightenment, the Dhamekha Stupa of Sarnath which commemorates his first sermon, and the Nirvana Temple of Kusinara which commemorates the Buddha's passing.

Inside the temple, the walls are covered with colorful hand-painted murals showing traditional Buddhist themes, including thirty-three detailed images along the upper walls depicting the life of the Buddha. The temple has few chairs and the open floor space is covered with a red carpet. At the front center of the large room there is an impressive altar with a golden statue of the Buddha sitting crossed-legged on top. The altar is adorned with religious objects and flowers. Outside the temple stand two sentinel sixteen-foot-tall Yakkha giants, and two big Nagas (royal serpents) lie along its main walkway.

The surrounding grounds are carefully landscaped with walkways, flower beds, trees, plants, and Buddhist symbols. All contribute to create a very peaceful place. The afternoon I visited the monastery I was greeted by the resident head monk, Than Chaokhun Phra Vijitrd-hammapani (known as Than Chokun Wijit). Than Chokun Wijit has been at the monastery since 1993 when it opened. He explained that the monks chose to build the monastery in the Orlando area because they wanted to bring the teachings of Buddhism to all, not just to Buddhists. This decision proved to be right because year after year the monastery continues to grow and attract people from all backgrounds. Several monks live at the monastery. He explained that Buddhist monks do not worship the Buddha. Instead they worship the spiritual awakening the Buddha found in his life. They practice daily chanting, prayer, medita-tion, and follow the Buddhist precepts. Some of the chanting is done in Pali, which is the language spoken by the Buddha. They live a simple life. Than Chokun Wijit thinks that part of the problem in society is the

Wat Florida Dhammaram Buddhist Temple, Kissimmee

63

need for material possessions. We always want more. The monks own nothing except for the clothes and sandals they wear. We spent more than two hours together strolling and talking about Buddhism, the practice of meditation, and the meaning of life. At the end of our talk, when it was time to go, I bowed to Than Chokun Wijit and thanked him for his time and patience. He nodded and said, "You learn fast." He then asked me to come back. As I drove home that evening, I couldn't help but wonder about the simple words of Than Chokun Wijit, and hoped that some day I would return to this special place of peace.

When entering the Wat Florida Dhammaram temple or its shrines it is the custom to take off your shoes and leave them outside. Buddhists believe the temple is pure and shoes are dirty. The monks are very friendly and always willing to teach about meditation and Buddhism to anyone. The monastery offers meditation practice and guidance daily. All are welcome regardless of faith background. No experience is needed.

The monastery has a few cabins available for overnight visitors. Overnight retreats are limited and have to be arranged ahead of

One of several shrines at Wat Florida Dhammaram

time. Donations are welcomed but not required. The Wat Florida Dhammaram monastery is open daily.

DIRECTIONS AND INFORMATION

Wat Florida Dhammaram's address is 2421 Old Vineland Road, Kissimmee, Florida 34746. Old Vineland Road is a side street off US 192 (about 1.5 miles east of the State Road 535 intersection).

For information call (407) 397-9552 or visit their informative website www.watflorida.org.

Spiritual Places in
South Florida

27

THE ANCIENT SPANISH
MONASTERY
Miami

$\mathcal{S}$ituated in north Miami Beach, the Ancient Spanish Monastery is perhaps one of the most unusual spiritual places in Florida. Although no monks live here any longer, the history of the monastery cloisters is nothing short of remarkable. Known originally as the Monastery of Saint Bernard de Clairvaux, it was built by Cistercian monks during the early twelfth century in Sacramenia, a town north of Segovia, in Spain. It was named after the famous Cistercian monk Bernard de Clairvaux, who was a very influential figure in the Catholic Church at the time. The monks lived in the monastery for seven hundred

Inside an authentic 12th century Cistercian monastery, Miami

years until it was seized and sold during the Spanish social revolution of the 1830s. In 1925, almost one hundred years later, American million-aire William Randolph Hearst bought the monastery cloisters and its surrounding buildings. The structures were taken apart stone by stone and packed into thousands of wooden crates for shipment to America. Due to financial problems he was having at the time, Hearst auctioned the collection upon its arrival, and the stones remained at a New York warehouse for twenty-six years. In 1952 the stones were purchased by W. Edgemon and R. Moss and brought to the present location with the idea to turn the cloisters into a tourist attraction. It took nineteen months to reassemble the monastery into its original form. Later, during the early 1960s, the Episcopal Church bought the property and today the monas-tery is owned by the Saint Bernard de Clairvaux Episcopal Church.

Standing in front of the monastery cloisters, you get a sense of going back in time. The sight is truly impressive. Here you are in south Florida looking at an authentic twelfth-century Spanish monastery. Walking inside the monastery's pre-Gothic-style hallways, it is easy to feel capti-vated by the architectural detail of its wall carvings, the long arched

The Ancient Spanish Monastery, Miami

columns, and the life-size statues. At the center of the cloisters is an enclosed garden patio with an ancient well made of Roman granite. The chapel, which originally was the monastery's refectory (dining hall), is used by the Saint Bernard de Clairvaux Episcopal Church. The baptismal font is over eight hundred years old and was used in the monastery church. High on the chapel's wall above the main altar are two unique round stained-glass windows. Outside, the monastery gardens are very peaceful with many trees, exotic plants, and paths. Beautiful statues adorn the lush grounds.

The Saint Bernard de Clairvaux Episcopal Church holds weekly services in the chapel. The Ancient Spanish Monastery is open daily to the public. A gift shop is located by the monastery entrance. Tours of the monastery are available. A small admission fee is required for the monastery. For schedule information contact the Ancient Spanish Monastery directly or check their website.

DIRECTIONS AND INFORMATION

The Ancient Spanish Monastery's address is 16711 W. Dixie Highway, Miami, Florida 33160. The monastery property is on the corner of N.E. 167th Street and W. Dixie Highway, just west of Biscayne Boulevard (US 1) and past the train tracks. The monastery entrance is half a block north of N.E. 167th Street.

For hours and information call (305) 945-1461 or visit their website www.spanishmonastery.com.

28

CAMPO
SAN JOSÉ
Lake Placid

*C*ampo San José is a Roman Catholic retreat center situated in Lake Placid in south Florida. Open since 1996, the retreat center is operated under the auspice of the Diocese of Venice. Campo San José was founded with the mission to be a place of prayer and spiritual renewal, especially for the Hispanic community. The retreat center provides a peaceful and beautiful atmosphere conducive to reflection and prayer.

Campo San José offers several scheduled retreats year-round, including youth seminars and marriage encounters. Group retreats are also available. The center has comfortable overnight facilities and provides meals.

For the latest event schedule, call the center directly or check their website. Campo San José is open to all denominations.

DIRECTIONS AND INFORMATION

Campo San José's address is 170 S. Sun 'n' Lake Boulevard, Lake Placid, Florida 33852. The retreat center is located near the south end of Grassy Lake. Sun 'n' Lake Boulevard runs off US 27. Lake Placid is about 100 miles south of Orlando and 35 miles northwest of Lake Okeechobee.

For information call (863) 385-6762 or visit their website www. camposanjose.com. Although the website is in Spanish, the staff is bilingual.

29

Cenacle Spiritual Life Center
Lantana

The Cenacle Spiritual Life Center is a lovely retreat center situated on ten acres in the Lantana area in Palm Beach County. The retreat center opened in 1962 and it is operated by the Cenacle Sisters, a Roman Catholic order that originated in France in 1826. The word Cenacle means "upper room," and in this case it refers to the room where Jesus celebrated the Last Supper with the Apostles, and where later Mary, the disciples, and the women awaited the coming of the Holy Spirit.

The retreat center sits on a beautiful waterfront property along the western side of the Intracoastal Waterway. As you come in the main entrance there is a long paved driveway. The registration desk is in the first building through the double doors. The center's chapel is located inside. A small bookstore that sells hard-to-find spirituality books is found here as well. Outside, there is a big labyrinth in front of the center. The Cenacle labyrinth is a replica of the famous Chartres Labyrinth in France. Walking the labyrinth is an ancient practice of meditation and prayer. It is said that circling to the center helps to clear the mind and can offer insights into one's own spiritual journey. The retreat's lush grounds are peaceful, with palm trees and several walkways through the property. The Intracoastal is visible around the back of the center. Here the view is quite scenic and relaxing. There are a few benches to sit down.

The Cenacle Sisters make vows of poverty, chastity, and obedience. The sisters strive to lead a life of prayer, community, and ministry sharing the word of God through retreats, spiritual direction, and religious education. For this, the Cenacle center offers a wide variety of retreats and programs throughout the year, many of them led by nationally and internationally known spiritual leaders. Some programs include the spiritual exercises of Saint Ignatius, contemplative prayer, meditation, spiritual support groups, and labyrinth prayer days. The Cenacle offers many scheduled retreats for women, men, and for all seekers. These cover a rich range of traditional and progressive spiritual topics and usually last from one to several days. Individual retreats are also available. These can be directed (meeting with a spiritual director) or private (on your own). For overnight stays, the Cenacle retreat center has single and double rooms available. All rooms are air-conditioned. Bathrooms are shared. Meals are provided for overnight retreats. The Cenacle is a nonprofit organization. For retreats there is a suggested donation to help cover the expenses of room and meals.

The Cenacle is a very active retreat center. For the latest retreat schedule, check their website or contact the center directly. If considering a retreat stay, call the center with plenty of advance time. The Cenacle Spiritual Life Center welcomes people from all denominations.

*The Cenacle Spiritual
Life Center, Lantana*

DIRECTIONS AND INFORMATION

The Cenacle Spiritual Life Center's address is 1400 S. Dixie Highway, Lantana, Florida 33462. The retreat center is located about one mile east of I-95. The entrance to the Cenacle center is on the east side of Dixie Highway (US 1), just north of Hypoluxo Road in Palm Beach County.

For information call (561) 582-2534 or visit their website www. cenaclesisters.org.

30

DUNCAN CONFERENCE CENTER
Delray Beach

*T*he Duncan Conference Center is a peaceful retreat facility located on more than five acres in Delray Beach in south Palm Beach County. The center has been open for several years and is administered by the Episcopal Church of Southeast Florida. The secluded grounds provide a welcoming atmosphere with colorful gardens, beautiful trees, and walking paths.

The retreat center's overnight accommodations include modern air-conditioned rooms with private bath. In order to minimize distractions, the guestrooms do not have phones or TVs. There are several meeting rooms, a dining room, a lovely chapel, and a bookstore that carries a good selection of books, music, and religious items. There is an outdoor brick labyrinth for prayer and meditation. Walking the labyrinth's rings to the center is an ancient tradition that it is believed to symbolize one's own spiritual journey to the center.

Duncan Conference Center offers retreats and scheduled events year-round. Retreats are available for groups, churches, families, couples, and individuals. For retreat information and availability contact the center directly or check their website. Duncan Conference Center is open to people of all denominations.

DIRECTIONS AND INFORMATION

The Duncan Conference Center's address is 15820 S. Military Trail, Delray Beach, Florida 33484. The center is just north of Linton Boulevard (Route 782) and about 2 miles west of I-95. Delray Beach is north of Boca Raton.

For information call (561) 496-4130 or visit their website www.duncancenter.org.

31

JEWISH MUSEUM
OF FLORIDA
Miami Beach

*T*he Jewish Museum of Florida is a unique place. Known as "the jewel of South Beach," the museum houses a large collection of hundreds of rare photographs, artifacts, and documents depicting Jewish history in Florida from 1763 to the present. The museum opened in 1995 after a two-year restoration of an abandoned Orthodox synagogue that once served Miami Beach's first Jewish congregation. Built in 1936 the museum building has a copper dome, a beautiful marble bimah (Torah reading platform), several art deco features, and

A historic place, Jewish Museum
of Florida, Miami Beach

76

eighty original stained-glass windows. The building is on the National Register of Historic Places.

Over the years the museum has become a major cultural attraction and source of information for people from all backgrounds in Florida. The museum maintains several temporary and permanent exhibits. Perhaps the most important one is MOSAIC: Jewish Life in Florida. This massive collection was once a traveling exhibit that visited thirteen cities from 1990 to 1994. The interest generated by MOSAIC was so big that it eventually became the museum's core exhibit.

Because the Jewish Museum of Florida is not a static institution but an evolving entity, it is always collecting, preserving, and interpreting new material evidence of the Jewish heritage in Florida. In addition to the exhibits, the museum has plenty more to offer, including films, historical timelines, a database of Jewish names, and many educational programs and lectures. A museum gift shop that sells books and souvenirs is also available.

When visiting the museum for the first time, consider taking one of the walking tours. The collections are so extensive and contain so much embedded history that it can take a long time to view and read all the material on your own. The tour guides can effectively provide more insight into the human stories behind the multiple exhibits and photographs. The museum is open daily except on Mondays and Jewish holidays. There is a small admission fee.

DIRECTIONS AND INFORMATION

The Jewish Museum of Florida's address is 301 Washington Avenue, Miami Beach, Florida 33139. The museum is located at the intersection of Washington Avenue and 3rd Street, just south of 5th Street (MacArthur Causeway) in Miami Beach.

For information call (305) 672-5044 or visit their website www. jewishmuseum.com.

32

MANRESA RETREAT HOUSE
Miami

anresa Retreat House is a tranquil retreat center situated in southwest Miami. Manresa Retreat House is an Ignatian spiritual center staffed by Jesuit priests. The Jesuits are a Roman Catholic order that was founded by Saint Ignatius of Loyola in the sixteenth century. Open since 1987, the center has been an important place of spiritual renewal for many individuals and families, especially among the Hispanic community of south Florida. Manresa Retreat House is named after the town of Manresa in Spain where it is said that Saint Ignatius of Loyola experienced his spiritual conversion.

Manresa Retreat House, Miami

The center sits on a five-acre lot in a quiet neighborhood away from the hustle and bustle of the big city to the east. The retreat center has several buildings, including a lovely chapel, a small bookstore, a dining room, and a few conference rooms. For overnight stays there are comfortable private rooms with bathrooms available. All are air-conditioned. Outside, the peaceful grounds are ideal for silent walks along the lush gardens or simple reflection under the shade of a tree. A beautiful statue of the Virgin of Fatima is located in the northwest area of the property.

Manresa Retreat House offers multiple scheduled retreats and ongoing programs year-round. Some of the events are conducted in Spanish. Because of the center's Jesuit roots there is an emphasis on Ignatian spirituality. Several times a year the Ignatian Spiritual Exercises are offered. Additionally there are retreats for couples, family retreats, youth retreats, and religious courses.

For the latest retreat and event schedule, call the center directly or check their website. When planning to attend a retreat make sure to call with plenty of advance time to ensure availability. Manresa Retreat House is open to all denominations.

DIRECTIONS AND INFORMATION

Manresa Retreat House's mailing address is P.O. Box 651512, Miami, Florida 33265. The retreat center's physical address is 12190 S.W. 56th Street, Miami, Florida. The center is located at the intersection of S.W. 56th Street (Miller Drive) and S.W. 122nd Avenue, about half a mile west after the Florida Turnpike overpass (Highway 821). The entrance is on S.W. 122nd Avenue.

For information call (305) 596-0001 or visit their website www.efjc. com. Although the website is in Spanish, the staff is bilingual.

33

MorningStar Renewal Center
Miami

*M*orningStar Renewal Center is a beautiful spiritual center located in south Miami. The retreat center is of Roman Catholic tradition but open to all denominations. Prior to May 2004 the retreat center was operated by the Dominican Sisters of Saint Catherine de Ricci and was known as the Dominican Retreat House. The sisters ran the popular retreat center for forty-three years inspiring and touching the lives of many people in south Florida.

MorningStar Renewal Center sits on a ten-acre lush lot in the midst of a quiet residential neighborhood. As you drive through the main gate

Entrance to the peaceful MorningStar Renewal Center, Miami

there is long asphalt driveway with big palm trees on both sides. The parking area is to the left around the back of the building. The retreat center has a chapel, a small library, dining room, and lounge. The overnight facilities include air-conditioned private rooms with shared bathrooms. Outside, the grounds surrounding the center are very spacious and welcoming. The lawns are meticulously maintained with flowers, several kinds of tropical trees, and long winding walkways. The area is an oasis of tranquility, perfect for strolling or just sitting silently under a tree listening to the sounds of nature. There is a statue of the Virgin Mary around the back of the property and the Stations of the Cross are found towards the front.

MorningStar Renewal Center offers scheduled retreats and programs year-round on various spiritual and religious topics. Many programs are day events for women, men, couples, youth, and families. Some events are ecumenical with different religions meeting together in unity. The center is open daily. For the latest retreat and program schedules, contact the center or check their website. MorningStar Renewal Center is open to groups and individuals of all faiths.

DIRECTIONS AND INFORMATION

MorningStar Renewal Center's address is 7275 S.W. 124th Street, Miami, Florida 33156. The retreat center is about a mile east of US 1 on S.W. 124th Street (Chapman Field Drive).

For information call (305) 238-4367 or visit their website www.morningstarrenewal.org.

34

MOTHER OF GOD
HOUSE OF PRAYER
Alva

Mother of God House of Prayer is a small retreat center located in the vicinity of the Caloosahatchee River in the quiet town of Alva. This beautiful retreat center was founded in 1982. Mother of God House of Prayer is of Roman Catholic orientation but open to all denominations.

The retreat center sits on a ten-acre wooded property with a creek. The scenic grounds are conducive to spiritual reflection and prayer. Mother of God House of Prayer offers scheduled spirituality seminars, and special events year-round. Overnight retreats are available as well in the form of private retreats, directed retreats, and group retreats. Spiritual direction is provided in directed retreats. The center has a few private bedrooms and full bathrooms with shower. Additionally, there is a screened heated swimming pool, a big wooden deck overlooking the creek, a small chapel, a library, and a nature path with the Stations of the Cross.

For the latest scheduled retreats and seminars call the center directly or check their website. Because overnight retreat space is limited call with plenty of advance time to ensure availability. Mother of God House of Prayer is a self-sustaining non-profit organization so most events ask for a suggested donation to help cover expenses. Mother of God House of Prayer is open to all.

DIRECTIONS AND INFORMATION
Mother of God House of Prayer's address is 17880 Cypress Creek Road, Alva, Florida 33920. The retreat center is located along the northern side

of the Caloosahatchee River just west of Alva (and east of Fort Myers). Cypress Creek Road runs off N. River Road (Route 78) about 12 miles east of I-75.

For information call (239) 728-3614 or visit their website www. moghop.com.

35

OUR LADY OF FLORIDA
SPIRITUAL CENTER
North Palm Beach

*O*ur Lady of Florida Spiritual Center is a unique retreat center overlooking the Intracoastal Waterway and Singer Island in North Palm Beach. Opened in 1962 as a Passionist monastery and retreat house, Our Lady of Florida ceased to be a monastery in 1992 but continued its ministry as a retreat house. Our Lady of Florida Spiritual Center is a Roman Catholic facility operated by members of the Passionist Order in collaboration with the Diocese of Palm Beach.

The Passionist Order was founded in mid-eighteenth century Italy by Paolo Danei, a priest who later became known as Saint Paul of the

Unique architecture at Our Lady of Florida Spiritual Center, North Palm Beach

Cross. Saint Paul of the Cross is considered by many to be one of the greatest mystics of the eighteenth century. He wanted the world to know about God's infinite love for all made known through the passion and death of Jesus. The Passionists make a vow to promote the living memory of the Passion of Christ. They strive to lead simple lives and dedicate themselves to evangelize and work with the poor and those in greater need. Intense contemplation and prayer are very important in the lives of the Passionists, and although many go out as missionaries, many also serve at parishes and spiritual centers.

Spread out over a twenty-six-acre area, including a quarter mile of scenic waterfront, Our Lady of Florida Spiritual Center offers a natural setting conducive to contemplation and spiritual inspiration. As you drive in the long driveway you immediately get a sense of calm. The center has several interconnected buildings designed by renowned Franciscan architect Brother Cajetan Baumann. The simple stone architectural lines of the buildings were intended to provide a prayerful and peaceful environment for all visiting the center. Our Lady of Florida has two chapels: a small chapel inside and a big chapel by the front entrance. The main chapel has a large side wall with many stained-glass windows that let the light in creating a colorful effect inside. The retreat center has a library area, a small gift shop that sells books and religious articles, and a few conference rooms available for meetings. There is a large cafeteria-style dining room. The meals are very good. There is a lovely enclosed garden with a fountain outside the dining room area. This is an ideal spot for quiet reading and meditation. For overnight stays Our Lady of Florida has plenty of air-conditioned and comfortable private guestrooms. Some rooms are equipped for people with special needs. Outside, the surrounding grounds are beautifully landscaped and spacious with green lawns, many plants, and a variety of native trees. The Stations of the Cross are located along the gardens between the stone altar and the waterfront. The stations are carefully positioned to form a big cross, which is easily visible from above.

Our Lady of Florida Spiritual Center hosts many retreats, seminars, and conferences year-round. Some of the programs offered include days of prayer, scripture study, women's retreats, men's retreats, couples' retreats, singles' retreats, and many other scheduled events.

Personal retreats are also available. These types of individual retreats can be directed which include some guidance from a spiritual director, or nondirected, which means that you are on your own. Our Lady of Florida is a nonprofit organization. Most events and retreats have a suggested offering to help cover expenses. Over the years many have come to this special spiritual place and have been touched by the experience. For the latest event schedule or to inquire about retreat dates, call the center directly or check their website. Our Lady of Florida Spiritual Center is open to all denominations.

DIRECTIONS AND INFORMATION

Our Lady of Florida Spiritual Center's address is 1300 U.S. Highway #1, North Palm Beach, Florida 33408. The retreat center is located a little over 3 miles east of I-95 on US 1. The center's entrance is about 0.3 miles south of PGA Boulevard (Route 786).

For information call (561) 626-1300 or visit their website www.ourladyofflorida.org.

36

OUR LADY OF MOUNT CARMEL SPIRITUAL CENTER
Miami

Our Lady of Mount Carmel Spiritual Life Center is a Catholic retreat center located in north Miami. The spiritual center was founded in 1991 under the direction of the Diocese of Miami. Discalced Carmelite friars oversee the center. The Discalced Carmelite order was founded by Saint Teresa of Avila in 1562. The Discalced Carmelite friars follow the inspiration of Saint Teresa of Avila and Saint John of the Cross. Discalced means "barefoot" or "wearing sandals." The Discalced Carmelites aim at leading an austere and contemplative life.

Our Lady of Mount Carmel Spiritual Life center sits on fourteen acres of beautiful parklike property with many trees and green areas. Several statues of saints, including Saint Teresa of Avila, adorn the gardens. The spiritual center has a lovely chapel, prayer room, library, and eating area. There are a small number of private guestrooms for overnight retreats.

The spiritual center offers retreats, seminars, and religious talks year-round. Many programs are in Spanish but some are in English, too. Private retreats are available with spiritual direction given upon request. Meals are provided for retreats. A donation fee is required per retreat visit to help cover the expenses of room and board.

For specific retreat availability and program schedules, contact the center directly or check their website. Overnight guestrooms are limited so call with plenty of advance time. Our Lady of Mount Carmel Spiritual Life Center is open to people of all denominations.

DIRECTIONS AND INFORMATION

Our Lady of Mount Carmel Spiritual Life Center's address is 18330 N.W. 12th Avenue, Miami, Florida 33169. The spiritual center is at the intersection of N.W. 12th Avenue and N.W. 183rd Street (Miami Gardens Drive) just east of the Florida Turnpike.

For retreat information, call (305) 654-9760. For general information, call (305) 654-9761 or visit their website www.carmelitasmiami.com. Although the website is in Spanish, the staff is bilingual.

37

OUR LADY OF PERPETUAL HELP
RETREAT CENTER
Venice

Our Lady of Perpetual Help is a retreat and spirituality center located in Venice. This tranquil retreat center opened in 1995. Our Lady of Perpetual Help is a Roman Catholic facility available to all denominations.

The retreat center has a very open layout with several small buildings spread out over a big area along the scenic Myakka River. As you enter the grounds there is a small sign on the left side of the road that reads Janua Coeli (Gate of Heaven). A little further is the Lake of the Blessed Sacrament, with several benches and a paved path around it. The Stations of the Cross path is found here. The administration office building and the dining hall are straight ahead up the road. The center maintains a small gift shop with religious articles and books. On the north side of the lake is the Saint Joseph Chapel. Inside the chapel there are six beautiful stained-glass windows depicting the story of the famous icon of Our Lady of Perpetual Help. The retreat center has a number of houses for overnight stay. These modern villas have private bedrooms, bathrooms, and are air-conditioned. Outside, the natural grounds are very peaceful with live oaks, palm trees, and plenty of shade. The lovely Rosary Walk is situated across from the statue of Holy Family and right next to the Myakka River. This is a great place for reflection, and the view of the river is first-rate.

Our Lady of Perpetual Help offers many spiritual programs, seminars, and scheduled retreats throughout the year. Special retreats and events can be prearranged for groups as well. For retreat schedules, call the center directly or check their website.

Directions and Information

Our Lady of Perpetual Help Retreat Center's address is 3989 S. Moon Drive, Venice, Florida 34292. The retreat center is about 4.5 miles from I-75 (at the Jacaranda Boulevard exit). Take Jacaranda Boulevard east to Border Road. Turn right on Border Road and go straight until it ends on S. Moon Drive (about 2.5 miles). Turn right on S. Moon Drive and continue for a little over a mile (you will bear left and cross I-75). The entrance to the center will be on the right.

For information call (941) 486-0233 or visit their website www.olph-retreat.org.

Stations of the Cross at Our Lady of
Perpetual Help Retreat Center, Venice

38

SAINT MARY STAR OF THE SEA SPIRITUAL CENTER
Key West

*T*he Saint Mary Star of the Sea Spiritual Renewal Center is located on the scenic island of Key West. The spiritual retreat center is a ministry of the Saint Mary Star of the Sea parish. Organized in 1852, Saint Mary Star of the Sea church is the oldest Roman Catholic parish in south Florida. Surrounded by the Atlantic Ocean and the Gulf of Mexico, the church was named Star of the Sea because it would shine its light of hope to the faithful. The present-day church was completed in 1905, and it is listed as a National and State Historical Site. Saint Mary Star of the Sea's unique architecture is of a Victorian Gothic style with high walls and an arched ceiling inside. A prominent stained-glass window depicting Our Lady Star of the Sea is found above the main altar. Situated adjacent to the church for many years was the convent of Mary Immaculate. The convent closed in 1983. The spiritual renewal center was established in 1993 in a section of what used to be the convent building. The retreat center's facilities include several comfortable private guestrooms, bathrooms, eating area, conference room, and the Divine Mercy Adoration chapel. The chapel is open twenty-four hours a day for meditation and prayer. Outside, a stone grotto with statues of Our Lady of Lourdes and Saint Bernadette is located on the grounds. The devotional grotto was built in 1922 by the sisters living at the convent. Many people come to pray here at this place of special sacredness and beauty. The surrounding gardens are very peaceful. A gift shop offering a wide selection of books, music, statues, and other religious items is also available on the church premises.

Saint Mary Star of the Sea Spiritual Renewal Center offers overnight group retreats as well as special events, and educational programs, including Bible study and religious classes. To make retreat arrangements or for more information, call the spiritual renewal center directly. Saint Mary Star of the Sea Spiritual Renewal Center is open to people of all denominations.

DIRECTIONS AND INFORMATION

Saint Mary Star of the Sea Spiritual Renewal Center's address is 724 Truman Avenue, Key West, Florida 33040. The church is at 1010 Windsor Lane in Key West. The church and spiritual center are within walking distance of each other.

For information call (305) 294-1018 or visit their website www.keywestcatholicparish.org.

39

SHIVA VISHNU TEMPLE OF SOUTH FLORIDA
Southwest Ranches

*T*he Shiva Vishnu Temple is a traditional Hindu temple located just west of Davie in Broward County. The beautiful temple opened in November 2001 after several years of construction and planning. Staffed by priests from India, the temple is dedicated to offering religious, educational, and cultural values to the Hindu community of South Florida. Hinduism is believed to be the world's oldest religion going back to 4000 b.c.e. or earlier. The Vedas (or wisdom) are the main Hindu scriptures. There are four Vedas, each consisting of collections of ancient sacred texts written in Sanskrit. The first

Shiva Vishnu Temple of South Florida, located west of Davie

93

and most important Veda is the Rigveda. This is a group of about one thousand hymns to various deities. The other Vedas are the Samaveda, the Yajurveda, and the Atharvaveda. The Shiva Vishnu Temple follows the tradition of Shiva Agama and Pancharathra Agama. Agamas are sacred texts. For Hindus Shiva and Vishnu are supreme deities or representations of God.

Driving through the main gates of the Shiva Vishnu Temple, one cannot help but feel awed by the unique appearance of the building ahead. Following the ancient Dravidian style architecture from South India, the temple has two Raja Gopurams (royal entrance towers) at the front and two Vimana Gopurams (central towers) at the rear. These are built over the shrines of Shiva and Vishnu, and have a lot of intricate stone carvings. Inside, the temple has several small shrines with statues of deities. Outside, the temple complex includes a community hall building used for special events, a library, a lunch room, and plenty of parking. The surrounding grounds are very peaceful and green with lush trees and plants.

The Shiva Vishnu Temple offers religious services and educational programs year-round. All people are welcome. The resident priests are very friendly and willing to share their traditions. When visiting, keep in mind that shoes must be removed before entering the temple. Shoe racks are available outside the building. Shorts, photography, and cell phones are not allowed inside the temple. The Shiva Vishnu Temple is open daily. For specific hours and programs call the temple directly or check their website.

DIRECTIONS AND INFORMATION
The Shiva Vishnu Temple of South Florida's address is 5661 Dykes Road, Southwest Ranches, Florida 33331. Dykes Road runs off Griffin Road (Route 818) about half a mile west of I-75 in the Davie area. The entrance to the temple is 1 mile south of Griffin Road.

For information call (954) 689-0471 or visit their website www.shivavishnu.org.

40

THE SHUL OF
BAL HARBOUR
Surfside

ocated just a block from the Atlantic Ocean in Surfside, the Shul of Bal Harbour is one of the country's most unique Orthodox synagogues. The Shul is an institution based on the philosophy of Chabad Lubavitch, a branch of Hasidism or Jewish mysticism that stresses the importance of religious study. The Chabad Lubavitch is a dynamic Jewish movement that started in the eighteenth century in the town of Lubavitch in Russia and later expanded to other parts of the world. The Shul of Bal Harbour is an impressive place that stands out for its simplicity and beauty. Its solid architecture derives from three famous synagogues in Poland: the Stara or Old Synagogue in Kazimierz, the Rema Synagogue in Krakow, and the Warsaw Great Synagogue.

The Shul or "House of G-d" is a spiritual center for all Jews in south Florida, including those returning to their Jewish roots as well as those already practicing the faith. For the Jewish community at large a shul is a house of gathering for prayer, a house for learning, a house for acts of kindness, and a minor holy temple. The Shul is also a meeting place for social, religious, cultural, and family events. The Shul strives to be a home away from home.

Besides the traditional synagogue services, the Shul offers many educational programs, including Torah study classes for beginner and advanced levels. To include the multi-ethnic community some programs are even taught in other languages such as Hebrew, Spanish, and German. Youth services and singles programs are available as well. A full-service Jewish library is open for study and research.

Although most events in the Shul are geared to the Jewish faithful, many are open to people of all faiths.

DIRECTIONS AND INFORMATION

The Shul of Bal Harbour's address is 9540 Collins Avenue, Surfside, Florida 33154. The town of Surfside is just north of Miami Beach. The Shul is located at the intersection of 95th Street and Collins Avenue.

For information call (305) 868-1411 or visit their website www. theshul.org.

41

WAT
BUDDHARANGSI
Miami

he Wat Buddharangsi is an impressive Buddhist monastery located on a five-acre site in the Redland area of south Miami. Founded by Thai monks, the Wat Buddharangsi sanctuary was established in order to offer a holy place of worship for Miami's Buddhist community. The Wat Buddharangsi monks practice Theravada Buddhism, the most traditional form of the Buddhist faith.

Although the Wat Buddharangsi goes back to the 1980s, the present-day temple and monastery buildings were completed in mid-2003 after several years of construction planning and work. Some of the buildings

Wat Buddharangsi Buddhist Temple, Miami

include an all-purpose hall, classrooms, a bell tower, and the beautiful temple. Inside, the temple is very open with no chairs. A soft red carpet extends from wall to wall. To the right there is a raised platform with a row of seats reserved for the resident monks. In front is the main altar with a tall golden cross-legged Buddha in the center surrounded with many religious objects.

Outside, the grounds are very pleasing with paved walkways, various kinds of trees, and lush green vegetation. There is a deep calmness and silence everywhere. Walking through the monastery gates, I couldn't help but notice the amazing contrast of the sight before me. Here was this magnificent sacred place of an Eastern spiritual tradition going back thousands of years in the middle of the serene rural landscape of southeast Florida.

Prayer, meditation, and worship are all important parts of Buddhism. The Wat Buddharangsi monastery is a place where one can do all of these. Keep in mind that before entering the Wat Buddharangsi temple or its buildings you must remove your shoes, according to Buddhist custom.

The monks offer several types of classes primarily on weekends, including meditation, Buddhist teachings, and Thai language. In addition, many traditional Buddhist ceremonies and festivals are celebrated throughout the year. All are welcome regardless of faith background. The Wat Buddharangsi monastery is open daily.

DIRECTIONS AND INFORMATION

Wat Buddharangsi's address is 15200 S.W. 240th Street, Miami, Florida 33032. The monastery site is located at the intersection of S.W. 240th Street and S.W. 152nd Avenue. The entrance is on S.W. 152nd Avenue about half a mile south of S.W. 232nd Street (Silver Palm Drive).

For information call (305) 245-2702 or visit their website www.watmiami.iirt.net.

Beyond Florida

(Spiritual Places Within a Day's Drive)

42

BLESSED TRINITY SHRINE RETREAT
Holy Trinity, AL

*B*lessed Trinity Shrine Retreat is a peaceful retreat center nestled on 1200 acres of woodlands bordering the Chattahoochee River in Holy Trinity, Alabama, near the Georgia border. The retreat center was founded in 1965 and is operated by sisters from the Missionary Servants of the Most Blessed Trinity. This Roman Catholic congregation of sisters was established in this location in 1918. Although the main congregation was forced to move to Philadelphia after their motherhouse building burned down in 1930, the sisters remained committed to their presence in Alabama. The congregation's wooden chapel survived the fire and is today known as the Shrine of the Blessed Trinity Chapel.

The center's grounds are very scenic with gardens, pond, trees, and ample green areas. The Stations of the Cross and a grotto are found here as well. There are wooded paths, perfect for quiet contemplative walks in a natural setting. The beautiful river is a two-mile stroll away.

The retreat center facilities include comfortable air-conditioned private guestrooms, a library, several meeting rooms, a cafeteria-style dining room, an indoor meditation garden, a modern chapel, and a gift store that carries books and religious articles. In addition, the center has a small hermitage house available for those desiring greater solitude. The hermitage has a bedroom, bathroom, kitchen, and prayer area.

Blessed Trinity Shrine Retreat offers many scheduled seminars and retreats year-round, including men's retreats, women's retreats, and group retreats. The seminars cover a wide range of spiritual topics. Individual directed and private retreats are also available. Spiritual direction is provided for directed retreats. With private retreats you are basically on your own. Meals are included for retreats. A donation is required per retreat stay to help cover the expenses of room and board.

To make a retreat inquiry or to get the latest schedule of events contact the center directly or check their website. Allow plenty of advance time when planning a private retreat visit. Blessed Trinity Shrine Retreat is open to people of all denominations.

DIRECTIONS AND INFORMATION
Blessed Trinity Shrine Retreat's mailing address is 107 Holy Trinity Road, Ft. Mitchell, Alabama 36856. The physical address is 107 Holy Trinity Road in Holy Trinity, Alabama. The town of Holy Trinity is about 20 miles south of Columbus, Georgia.

For information call (334) 855-4474 or visit their website www.msbt. org.

43

EMMANUEL RETREAT HOUSE
Greenville, SC

*E*mmanuel Retreat House is a quiet retreat center located in Greenville, South Carolina. The retreat center is maintained by the Monastery of Saint Clare, a Roman Catholic institution of the Poor Clares sisters. The retreat house is situated next to the monastery. Although the Monastery of Saint Clare was founded in 1954, Emmanuel Retreat House did not open until the early 1970s. Initially it was a retreat center for sisters, but later during the mid 1980s it welcomed all women. The Poor Clares sisters are a cloistered branch of the Franciscan Order. Following the inspiration of their founders, Saint Clare and Saint Francis of Assisi, the sisters lead a contemplative life of prayer, poverty, and community.

Emmanuel Retreat House offers group and private retreats for women year-round. Retreats can be for the day or overnight. Spiritual direction is provided upon request. The retreat house has a few private rooms for overnight stay. In addition there are a sitting area, an eating area, and a kitchen where guests can prepare their own food. The chapel is within walking distance from the house. Retreatants are invited to join the sisters in the prayers and the Liturgy of the Hours in the chapel or can follow their own schedule of prayer, reading, and meditation. A donation fee per retreat is suggested to help cover expenses of room and board.

For retreat availability, contact the monastery center directly. Because overnight space is limited allow plenty of advance time. Emmanuel Retreat House is open to women of all denominations.

DIRECTIONS AND INFORMATION

Emmanuel Retreat House's address is 1916 N. Pleasantburg Drive, Greenville, South Carolina 29609. The retreat house is in a cul-de-sac that backs up to the Monastery of Saint Clare.

For information call (864) 244-4514 or visit their website www. poorclaresc.com.

44

EPWORTH BY THE SEA
St. Simons Island, GA

*E*pworth By The Sea is a large retreat complex situated on eighty-three acres of scenic riverfront along the banks of the Frederica River on St. Simons Island. Built on what used to be part of a prosperous lumber mill plantation, the retreat center opened in 1950 and it is operated by the South Georgia Conference of the United Methodist Church. Epworth got its name in honor of the childhood home in England of John and Charles Wesley. Both brothers visited St. Simons Island several times in 1736. John Wesley is the founder of the Methodist Church.

Entrance to Epworth By The Sea Methodist Center

As I drove past the main gate, the first thing I noticed was the postcardlike appearance of the grounds with their giant live oaks, palm trees, and spacious green lawns. From the entrance the beautiful chapel is visible to the right. This wooden chapel was originally built for the people working at the lumber mill. The Lovely Lane Chapel is named after the place in Baltimore where Francis Asbury, the first Methodist bishop in America, was ordained in 1784. Weekly worship services, meditation, and special events are still held in the historic chapel. The center's reception office is a little further on the left side. The dining room and gift shop are located in this building as well. Almost directly across from the office building is the Moore Museum. The museum offers lots of information about the area, its unique history, and the Methodist faith. A self-guided tour and video are available. A special collection library is housed in the same building.

Epworth is a peaceful place with many walkways and gardens. A water fountain is found near the Strickland auditorium building. The prayer tower building is located close to the river. This unusual struc-

The prayer tower on the Frederica River, Epworth By The Sea, St. Simons Island

ture is visible from far away and has a big cross on top. From here the view of the Frederica River is spectacular.

Epworth offers both scheduled retreats as well as private retreats (on your own). Many types of retreatants visit throughout the year, including large groups, churches, families, and individuals. For this, Epworth center has motel-style buildings with comfortable rooms. The rooms have air-conditioning, private bathroom, TV, and some have a phone. In addition, there are family apartments, youth cabins, and several recreation facilities available, including tennis courts, athletic fields, swimming pool, preschool nursery, and playground to name a few. Two small fishing piers are located on the waterfront.

Epworth's mission is to provide a Christian place for worship, study, and fellowship. Epworth By The Sea is a great place for those seeking time apart in a friendly welcoming atmosphere.

Directions and Information
Epworth By The Sea's address is 100 Arthur J. Moore Drive, St. Simons Island, Georgia 31522. The retreat center is located about half a mile from the St. Simons Island causeway (Demere Road). From Demere Road go north on Sea Island Road and make the first left on Hamilton Road. Go straight until you come to Arthur J. Moore Drive. Gascoigne Bluff Park is across to the left. Go right on Arthur J. Moore Drive. The entrance to Epworth is a couple hundred yards ahead.

For information call (912) 638-8688 or visit their website www. epworthbythesea.org.

45

MONASTERY OF THE HOLY SPIRIT
Conyers, GA

*O*ur Lady of the Holy Spirit Monastery is a Roman Catholic monastery of the Cistercian Order of the Strict Observance (OCSO), also known as Trappist. The Trappists are reformed Cistercians, who are reformed Benedictines. But all three orders follow the Rule of St. Benedict, considered to be the father of monasticism in the west.

Nestled among the rolling hills of north central Georgia, the Monastery of the Holy Spirit is one of the Southeast's most inviting spiritual places. The moment that you get off Highway 212 and turn into the monastery entrance you feel an overwhelming sense of natural beauty

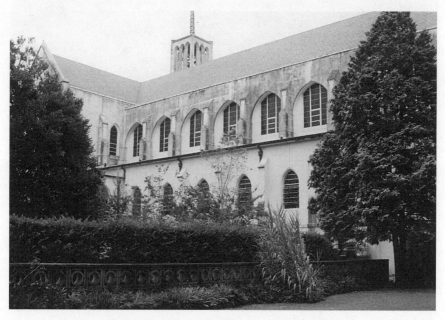

Monastery of the Holy Spirit, Conyers, Georgia

and peace. The narrow entrance road is paved and lined with magnolia trees on both sides. After about a quarter mile the road opens and you see the first monastery buildings. The small building straight ahead is the welcome center. To the right are the Abbey Store and the bonsai nursery. The cloistered area buildings are behind the welcome center but are closed to visitors. The beautiful Abbey Church and retreat house are to the left of the welcome center. If you are going to the retreat house, follow the signs posted along the entrance. A small lake can be seen to the left of the retreat area. The monastery grounds are surrounded with tall trees, colorful gardens, and walking trails. There is a tremendous air of serenity and silence. Although you can hear birds and other soft sounds, there are no urban noises. The monastery was founded in 1944 by a group of Trappist monks sent with this mission from the Monastery of Gethsemani in Kentucky. The present-day Abbey Church, bell tower, and monastery buildings were completed in the 1960s. The architecture is solid and simple. The inside of the church is impressive without being ostentatious. It has high arches and a large round stained-glass window

View inside the beautiful church at the
Monastery of the Holy Spirit

depicting the Madonna and the Child Jesus above the main altar. The original wooden monastery structures, including a barn where the monks first lived, are still standing, but they are no longer used. These are located to the right of the cloister buildings.

The number of monks living in the monastery fluctuates from time to time. Although some of the monks are priests, many are not, but all are brothers dedicated to lead a life of contemplation and worship of God. According to the monastic tradition, the life of a monk consists of *ora et labora,* or work and prayer. The day is divided between private prayer and meditation, communal prayer, Mass, and physical work within the community. The monks follow a strict schedule of prayer each day. Several prayer services are held in the Abbey Church and are open to the public: Vigils (before sunrise), Lauds (morning prayer) with Mass, Vespers (evening prayer), and Compline (night prayer).

The Monastery of the Holy Spirit offers many scheduled retreats throughout the year open to both men and women of all faiths. These usually include a combination of time for prayer, solitude, quiet recreation, and attending talks on various spiritual topics. Additionally, private retreats are offered as needed and as space is available. These self-directed retreats provide the most time alone since basically you are on your own, although spiritual direction is always available upon request. If you have never been on a spiritual retreat before, perhaps the scheduled retreat may be better suited for you.

My first overnight retreat at the Monastery of the Holy Spirit was a scheduled three-day retreat held Friday through Sunday. The experience was magnificent and very spiritually enriching. I recall arriving in the late afternoon and walking up the old brick steps from the retreat area parking lot. There is a garden on one side and a low brick wall along the path to the retreat building entrance. The white three-story retreat house is connected to the side of the Abbey Church. I found that in order to really experience the spiritual life of the monks one should attend, at least for a day, each of the prayer services. This includes Vigils which means getting up around 3:30 a.m. to be in the Abbey Church by 4 a.m. I remember sitting in the dimly lit church alongside monks singing verses of the Psalms, waiting for the monks on the other side to respond, and feeling that these were truly spiritual men. I know that I felt the presence of God that night in the Abbey Church.

Silence is one of the most important aspects of monastic tradition. While in the monastery, guests are asked to follow this rule and restrict talking to designated areas and times. It was an eye-opening experience when I had my first silent meal. Actually I enjoyed it because it made me pay more attention to the act of eating, which for many of us has become so automatic. If you are looking for a quiet outdoor space, there is a beautiful meditation garden outside the retreat house eating area. Monks are very friendly and in many ways are more similar to us than different. One day going up the retreat house stairs I noticed the cemetery behind the Abbey Church. I asked Brother Michael about it, and he said that that was the only way out of the monastery for him. I counted several rows of white crosses. Over the years I have visited the Monastery of the Holy Spirit several times, and every time has been a uniquely wonderful spiritual experience. But it is an experience that words cannot fully describe and each person must seek for himself or herself.

When planning to schedule a retreat at the Holy Spirit Monastery keep in mind that there is limited space, so try to call with plenty of advance time. Married couples can be accommodated. For the most part, retreats go Monday through Thursday or Friday through Sunday. Of course, there are exceptions to this, and the monks will do their best to accommodate your retreat requests. With a little flexibility on your part, they will most likely find an available date for you. Saint Benedict tells in his Monastic Rule that all guests should be received as Christ. Although the monastery does not charge a fee for retreats, there is a suggested donation per day to help cover the expenses of room and meals. The rooms in the retreat house are austere but comfortable with a bed, desk, and a chair. All rooms have heat and air-conditioning, and some have a sink. Most rooms share a bathroom and shower with the room next door. There are floor showers and bathrooms too. The food is very good and healthy. Casual clothes are allowed within the monastery, but no shorts. It is best to be mindful of the monastic atmosphere. Finally, if you go make sure to visit the bonsai nursery and the Abbey

Store known in the surrounding area for its religious articles, books, music, and delicious fruitcakes handmade by the monks.

DIRECTIONS AND INFORMATION

The Monastery of the Holy Spirit's address is 2625 Highway 212 S.W. (Browns Mill Road), Conyers, Georgia 30094. The monastery is a few miles south of I-20 and about 30 miles southeast of Atlanta. The monastery is open daily.

For general information call (770) 483-8705. For retreat questions, including schedules, call the retreat house at (770) 760-0959. For all of the above visit their website www.trappist.net.

46

IGNATIUS HOUSE
JESUIT RETREAT CENTER
Atlanta, GA

*I*gnatius House is a tranquil retreat center situated on twenty acres of scenic hillside overlooking the Chattahoochee River. Located in the Sandy Springs suburb of Atlanta, Ignatius House is staffed by the Jesuit fathers and brothers of the Southern Province of the Society of Jesus.

The center has been operating for many years offering the community a place for spiritual growth and guidance through retreats and teaching, including the practice of the Ignatian spiritual exercises. The spiritual exercises include silent reflection, meditation, and praying the

Retreat building at Ignatius House Jesuit Retreat Center, Atlanta, Georgia

scriptures. They are based on the notes that Saint Ignatius himself kept as he experienced his own spiritual conversion in the sixteenth century at Manresa, Spain. Saint Ignatius of Loyola founded the Roman Catholic Jesuit Order in the year 1540. The Jesuits commit themselves to the vows of poverty, chastity, and obedience.

The Ignatius House Center is not visible from the road (Riverside Drive). As you turn into the main entrance, the driveway goes up and veers right before you see the buildings. The retreat house is the two-story building at the right end of the parking lot. Inside are plenty of comfortable air-conditioned rooms for overnight stays. Each room has a private bath, a desk and a chair. There is a cozy dining room on the first floor with a view of the gardens and water fountain. A small library is also available. Outside, across from the front parking lot, is the center's bookstore/gift shop. Here you can find an interesting selection of books, music, and religious articles. The Jesuits' residence is the house located past the bookstore to the right.

A lovely outdoor chapel sits on the small hilltop across from the retreat building. The access path is off to the right of the parking lot.

Entrance to Ignatius House Jesuit Retreat Center, Atlanta, Georgia

Follow

Follow the signs. Above the chapel's roof a huge tower extends high up with a cross visible from far away. Below the roof, a beautiful stained-glass cross hangs from the center. A gracious stone wall with religious symbols and depictions surrounds the chapel grounds. The area is very quiet and welcoming to reflection and prayer.

The property grounds are very relaxing and pleasing with lush vegetation, trees, and several peaceful trails. The Stations of the Cross are placed along the walking trail behind the retreat house. A three-tiered wooden deck located on the edge of the bluff above the Chattahoochee River offers a spectacular view of the natural surroundings. There are chairs and benches where you can sit and reflect in nature. From the deck you can take the stairs down to the banks of the river and walk around to the nearby creek.

The Jesuits seek to find God in all things and believe that we must exercise spiritually for our spiritual health. Ignatius House is dedicated to offering spiritual retreats for all people seeking to discover God's presence in their lives. There are many types of retreats offered year-round, including women's retreats, men's retreats, married couples' retreats, and the spiritual exercises retreats. Most retreats are scheduled and open to both groups and/or individuals. Overnight retreats usually last two or three days, but there are a few longer ones too. There is no set fee for overnight retreats. Although there is a suggested donation per stay, people are asked to give what they can to help cover the cost of room and meals. Retreats at Ignatius House fill up fast so whether you are considering a spiritual retreat or just need a little time away from the daily routine, contact the center with plenty of advance time. Ignatius House is open to people of all denominations.

Directions and Information
Ignatius House's address is 6700 Riverside Drive N.W., Atlanta, Georgia 30328. The entrance to the retreat center is located on Riverside Drive about 1.8 miles north of the I-285 exit and half a mile before the intersection with Johnson Ferry Road.

For retreat information call (404) 255-0503 or visit their website www.ignatiushouse.org.

47

MEPKIN
ABBEY
Moncks Corner, SC

*A*bbey of Our Lady of Mepkin is a Roman Catholic monastery of the Cistercian Order of the Strict Observance (OCSO), also known as Trappist. Although the present-day Abbey Church, library, and monastery buildings were built between 1993 and 2001, Mepkin Abbey was founded in 1949 by a group of twenty-nine monks sent from the Monastery of Gethsemani in Kentucky with this purpose.

Located in the scenic Lowcountry region in the vicinity of Moncks Corner and alongside the west branch of the Cooper River, Mepkin Abbey is a stunningly beautiful place to visit or spend a few days in a spiritual retreat. The name Mepkin is a Native American word which means "serene and lovely," and, true to its name, Mepkin Abbey is truly peaceful and lovely. As you turn into the monastery entrance (Mepkin Abbey Road) you will go along a line of magnificent Spanish moss–draped live oaks on both sides of the paved road. After about a quarter of a mile you will see the sign to the Reception Center house on the left. This is the best place for first-time visitors and guests to get information about the monastery and its rules. The Reception Center is also Mepkin's Abbey Store where you can find many items of monastic tradition, including specialty food, books, music, handcrafted art, religious articles, and the area's famous Mepkin Abbey fresh eggs.

The Abbey Church and monastery buildings are located a little further past the Reception Center area. Continue on the entrance road until you come to a three-way crossroads. The gardens are straight ahead. The farm (off-limits to visitors) is to the right, and the church and monastery buildings are to the left. Take the left road and go straight until you come to the visitors parking area. From the parking lot you will see the library building in front. The Abbey Church is right behind. The monks' cloistered area is right next to the church so try to be mindful of this and obey the posted signs. When in doubt ask before venturing on your own.

To the left of the Abbey Church's entrance is the lovely Bell Tower which symbolizes the seven voices of all who have lived in the land of Mepkin Abbey: the American Indians, the Laurens family, the African-American slaves, the Luce family, the friends and relatives buried here, the monastic community in glory, and the monastic community on the way.

The modern exterior look of the Abbey Church is sleek with straight lines but simple, not ostentatious. The inside of the abbey maintains the Trappist tradition of austerity with a combination of natural elements of wood, stone, tile, and high plain walls. The original monastery buildings and church do not exist anymore and once stood in the same area where the present-day buildings are located.

The monastery grounds are filled with lush vegetation, colorful flowers, ample meadows, and a variety of big trees. There are many winding paths that allow you to meander around and get a close look at the beauty of the surroundings. The Nancy Bryan Luce Gardens are located past the abbey buildings, next to the river. The gardens are very beautiful and offer an incredibly tranquil and secluded atmosphere. Several of the Luce family members are buried there in a small private graveyard. As you walk down the steps into the gardens, a statue of Our Lady of Mepkin holding the Child Jesus (built in 1954) stands to the right of the entrance. From this point the spectacular view of Cooper River is just a few yards away. This is the area of the river where once existed several rice fields when Mepkin was a rice plantation.

Following Saint Benedict's Monastic Rule, the Trappist monks at Mepkin Abbey lead a life dedicated to seek God through Christ. Communal prayer, solitude, manual work, and contemplation are some of the core monastic values that the brothers have chosen to follow. Visiting Mepkin I found an astounding feeling of silence and peacefulness. I felt quickly at ease and at home. I felt I was in God's place. At Mepkin Abbey the presence of the spiritual is noticeably real, inviting one to seek solitude and contemplation. I was there for only three days but left refreshed with a strong sense of inner peace and a desire to return someday to this lovely and serene place by the river.

Mepkin Abbey Monastery offers private retreats throughout the year. These are open to both men and women of all faiths. Married couples can also be accommodated upon request. Retreats are scheduled from Monday through Friday and from Friday through Monday. Week-long retreats are available by request. If you are interested in planning a retreat, make sure to reserve well in advance because space is very limited. Group day events can be scheduled with the guestmaster. All day visitors are encouraged to check in at the Reception Center upon arrival. Daily guided tours of the Abbey Church are offered from the Reception Center. Additionally, a special Monastic Guest program for men offers the opportunity to spend a period of thirty days (or longer with approval) living within the monastic community. These monastic guests must participate in all activities and obligations of the monks, including prayer and work. The Monastic Guest program requires advance reservations and is limited to a few men at a time.

Reception Center, Mepkin Abbey, South Carolina

Retreatants at Mepkin Abbey stay at one of several guest cabins located throughout the monastery grounds. The rooms are air-conditioned and very comfortable with a bed, desk, chair, and private bathroom with shower. Bed linens, towels, and basic toiletries are provided. You only need to bring your personal items. The retreatants follow the same meal schedule as the monks and eat in a guest area adjacent to the refectory (monks' dining room). The food is very good and healthy. During meals retreatants are asked to observe silence just as the monks do. The retreatants' dining facility stays open all day. Here you may find coffee, tea, hot chocolate, water, and fruits. All is self-service.

Daily prayer is an essential aspect of monastic life. Retreatants can attend all prayer services in the Abbey Church and are invited to participate in the Liturgy of the Hours (daily prayer cycle) with the monks, sitting alongside in a designated section of the choir. The Abbey Church is always open to guests. The monastery's Clare Boothe Luce Library located across from the Abbey Church is open to guests during designated times. Here you will find a vast collection with thousands of works on theology, monastic studies, philosophy, scripture, and liturgy.

The Clare Boothe Luce Library, Mepkin Abbey

Although usually there are no scheduled conferences during retreats, spiritual guidance is available upon request. Following the Benedictine tradition Mepkin Abbey does not charge guests for staying overnight but a suggested donation per day is expected to help cover room and board. Since Mepkin Abbey is a self-sustained community, these and other donations are greatly appreciated.

DIRECTIONS AND INFORMATION

Mepkin Abbey's address is 1098 Mepkin Abbey Road, Moncks Corner, South Carolina, 29461. The monastery entrance is off Dr. Evans Road about 6 miles south of SC 402. Mepkin Abbey is located about 40 miles northwest of Charleston.

For general information, including retreat availability, call (843) 761-8509 or visit their website www.mepkinabbey.org.

48

ORATORY CENTER FOR SPIRITUALITY
Rock Hill, SC

*E*stablished in 1934 the Rock Hill Oratory was the first Oratory center in the United States. Located on several acres in a tranquil residential area of Rock Hill, South Carolina, the Oratory is a Roman Catholic congregation of priests and brothers. The order was founded in 1575 in Italy by the popular Saint Philip Neri, known for his spontaneity, cheerfulness, and sometimes unconventional ways of bringing people to God. Saint Philip stressed love, humor, humility, and prayer among his followers. The members of the Congregation of the Oratory (CO) do not take traditional vows like other religious orders do. Instead the members come together by love and respect. The entire community is governed democratically, with all members having a voice in decisions. Oratorians serve at many places, including parishes, schools, and retreat centers.

The Rock Hill Oratory Center for Spirituality has been operating for many years, offering scheduled group retreats and ongoing programs to all those seeking to grow spiritually. Some of programs include Oratory prayer, Bible study, youth events, and varied religious seminars. Private retreats are available as well. These can be directed, which include meeting with a spiritual director, or unguided, in which direction is not provided. A fee per retreat event is required to help cover the expenses of room and board.

The retreat facilities include air-conditioned private rooms with bathrooms. There is a comfortable dining area available. The Oratory has a beautiful church and the surrounding grounds are quite peaceful. A prayer labyrinth is found outside. Walking the circles of the labyrinth is an ancient practice of prayer. Prayer is very important for Oratorians. They believe that through prayer our special gifts and talents are realized. The Rock Hill Oratory is a place of prayer where guests can feel closer to God.

For specific retreat information or to get the latest schedule of events, contact the Oratory directly or check their website. The Rock Hill Oratory Center for Spirituality is open to people of all denominations.

DIRECTIONS AND INFORMATION

The Rock Hill Oratory Center for Spirituality's address is 434 Charlotte Avenue, Rock Hill, South Carolina 29730. The retreat center is on Charlotte Avenue south off Cherry Road (west of I-77).

For information call (803) 327-2097 or visit their website www. rockhilloratory.com.

49

SACRED HEART
MONASTERY
Cullman, AL

acred Heart Monastery is a Roman Catholic monastery located in Cullman in northern Alabama. The monastery was founded in 1902 by Benedictine sisters that were sent to educate the children of Catholic immigrants in the area. Over the years the sisters successfully carried out this ministry, teaching many throughout the schools in the region. Following the Rule of Saint Benedict, the sisters lead a simple life dedicated to seeking God through prayer, community, and ministry. Because communal prayer is an essential aspect of monastic life, the sisters follow the Liturgy of the Hours, praying together in the church several times each day. The Eucharist is celebrated during this time as well.

Sacred Heart Monastery is not only beautiful, but it is also a peaceful place. The church and monastery building's Gothic architecture is solid and simple. The surrounding grounds with many trees, open lawns, and paths provide a natural setting conducive to outdoor contemplation and prayer.

Sacred Heart Monastery offers many scheduled spiritual retreats and conferences year-round. There are women's retreats, singles' retreats, and group retreats covering a wide range of spiritual topics. Private individual retreats are available too. These can be directed, which offer the opportunity to meet with a spiritual director, or self-directed, which means that you are on your own. The overnight facilities include comfortable private and shared guestrooms. Meals are provided. During retreats guests are encouraged to attend the Liturgy of the Hours and to celebrate the Eucharistic Liturgy with the sisters in the church.

Sacred Heart Monastery has a vocation program for single women discerning the call to religious life, as well as an oblate program. Oblates are lay Christian men and women who seek to lead a spiritual life deeply rooted in God. Oblates meet for an annual retreat at the monastery.

For the latest schedule of retreats and events, call the monastery directly or check their website. Keep in mind that overnight space is limited so allow plenty of advance time when planning a retreat. There is a suggested donation per retreat stay to help cover the expenses of room and board. Sacred Heart Monastery is open to people from all faiths.

DIRECTIONS AND INFORMATION

Sacred Heart Monastery's address is 916 Convent Road, Cullman, Alabama 35055. Convent Road runs north off Highway 278 a couple of miles east of I-65.

For general information call (256) 734-4622 or for retreat information call (256) 734-8302. The monastery's website is www.shmon.org.

50

SAINT BERNARD
ABBEY
Cullman, AL

Saint Bernard Abbey is a Roman Catholic monastery situated just south of Cullman in the beautiful Appalachian foothills of northern Alabama. The monastery was founded in 1891 by Benedictine monks sent from Saint Vincent's Abbey in Pennsylvania to minister to the German Catholic settlers in the area.

The Benedictine monks follow the teachings of Saint Benedict, an Italian monk born in the late fifth century who wrote the rule for monastic life and is considered to be the father of Christian monasticism in the West. The rule provides the foundation for the monk's life of prayer and work. At Saint Bernard Abbey the monks live in a community of brothers guided by an abbot and dedicated to seeking union with God through daily worship, spiritual reading, meditation, private prayer, and labor. Some of the Benedictine monks are priests and some are not, but all are brothers in Christ.

Since its foundation Saint Bernard Abbey has been actively involved in the community by ministering to parishes, maintaining a retreat center, and through education. Over the years the abbey has administered several schools on campus, including Saint Bernard Preparatory School which opened in 1981. This is a coed boarding and day school for grades 9–12. The monastery operates the famous Ave Maria Grotto. This is a four-acre landscaped park located on the monastery grounds that features 125 miniature cement and stone replicas of some of the world's most famous historic buildings and shrines. The replicas were hand-crafted over a period of forty-six years by Brother Joseph Zoettl, a German-born Benedictine monk who lived at the abbey for over sixty years. Some of the reproductions include the buildings of the Holy Land,

Saint Peter's Basilica, the Spanish missions of the Southwest, and the shrines of Lourdes and Fatima.

Saint Bernard Abbey has a long tradition of welcoming guests and visitors. The monastery offers scheduled group retreats, individual retreats, monastic guest retreats, vocation retreats, and special programs year-round. There are a limited number of private rooms available in the abbey building for monastic guests. The overnight abbey rooms are air-conditioned and some share a common bathroom. These are open to men, women, and married couples. There is a separate hospitality retreat center building (Boniface Hall) located within the monastery grounds. This facility is open to groups, individuals, and monastic guests. The hospitality retreat center has comfortable air-conditioned rooms with twin beds, private bathroom, and telephone. A few of these rooms are equipped for special needs. The hospitality center also has several conference rooms available. The monastery has a dining hall that provides complete meal service. Monastic guests eat their meals with the monks. Some meals are eaten in silence. In addition, monastic guests are encouraged to participate in the daily prayers of the Hours of Divine Office and celebrate Mass with the monks in the Abbey Church.

The monastery grounds, which cover eight hundred acres of wooded area, are very peaceful and offer plenty to see. There are many nature trails and ideal places for walking and quiet contemplation outdoors.

When planning a retreat at Saint Bernard Abbey it is recommended to call with plenty of advance time to ensure availability. To help cover expenses, a suggested donation is greatly appreciated. Both the monastery and the Ave Maria Grotto are open daily. For hours call the monastery or check their website. Saint Bernard Abbey is open to people from all denominations.

DIRECTIONS AND INFORMATION
Saint Bernard Abbey's address is 1600 Saint Bernard Drive SE, Cullman, Alabama 35055. The abbey is off highway US 278 a few miles east of I-65.

For general information call (256) 734-8291, or for retreat information call (256) 734-3946. The abbey's website is www.stbernardabbey.com.

51

SEA OF PEACE
HOUSE OF PRAYER
Edisto Island, SC

*S*ea of Peace House of Prayer is a peaceful Dominican retreat house located on Edisto Island, one of the barrier islands of South Carolina. Operated by Adrian Dominican sisters, the small retreat center opened in 1995 to support and encourage women in their spiritual journey. The center is in a secluded scenic setting overlooking the tidal marsh creek. The grounds are full of rich wildlife with many birds, and vegetation, including big live oaks and palmettos. There are wooded paths and a seven-circuit prayer labyrinth for quiet meditation. The center's facilities include a small number of private guestrooms, library, sunroom, and sitting areas. With the ocean nearby, the center is an oasis of tranquility and natural beauty.

Sea of Peace House of Prayer offers private retreats. Retreats can be on your own or directed, which includes guidance by a spiritual director. Retreatants can join the sisters for morning and evening prayers and during meals. A donation per retreat is required to help cover expenses of room and board.

For retreat availability and specific information contact the center directly. Overnight retreat space is limited so allow plenty of advance time. Sea of Peace House of Prayer is open to all denominations.

DIRECTIONS AND INFORMATION

Sea of Peace House of Prayer's address is 59 Palmetto Pointe, Edisto Island, South Carolina 29438. The retreat center is near Edisto Beach State Park. Edisto Island is just south of Charleston.

For information call (843) 869-0513 or visit their website www. seaofpeace.org.

52

SHRINE OF THE MOST BLESSED SACRAMENT
Hanceville, AL

Nestled among 380 acres of scenic countryside, the Shrine of the Most Blessed Sacrament is a unique spiritual place. Situated on the grounds of the Our Lady of the Angels Monastery in Hanceville, Alabama, the massive shrine church stands as a temple of peace and silence. The Poor Clare Nuns of Perpetual Adoration, a Roman Catholic order of cloistered nuns, live at the monastery and oversee the shrine. The Poor Clare nuns are an order of Franciscans sisters dedicated to loving God and leading simple lives. Although the shrine and monastery were completed in 1999, the Our Lady of the Angels Monastery was originally established in 1962 in Birmingham. The Shrine of the Most Blessed Sacrament was the inspiration of Mother Angelica, the popular nun and host of the Catholic EWTN television network, who wanted to build a house of prayer dedicated to the divine child Jesus. Mother Angelica is the founder of the Our Lady of the Angels Monastery in Birmingham.

Everything at the shrine grounds is impressive from the long winding entrance road, the solid yet simple thirteenth-century Roman-esque-Gothic architecture of the buildings, to the beautiful marble statue of the child Jesus in center of the piazza. One feels truly in a holy place. The shrine itself is a work of art built with the finest materials and craftsmanship. Bronze doors, high arched ceilings, marble floor patterns, stained-glass windows, and marble altars are just a few of the features to admire.

Outside the shrine church there is much to see. Castle San Miguel, a replica of a medieval castle, has a lovely gift shop with a wide selection of religious articles and books. The Creche or Holy Cave is a small chapel with a near life-size nativity scene. The chapel is a place of meditation on the wonders and mystery of Christmas. The Stations of the Cross are found between the arches along the south colonnade by the piazza.

The Shrine of Most Blessed Sacrament is a place where many people come for the day. At the present time there are no lodging accommodations at the shrine, but scheduled group pilgrimages are available. These are prearranged trips to the shrine with a group and include spiritual talks and tours of the shrine. Pilgrims may stay at one of the guesthouses or hotels nearby. If space is available, you can join one of the prescheduled groups, or you can plan your own group pilgrimage. For more specific visiting information, contact the shrine directly or check their website.

The Shrine of the Most Blessed Sacrament is open daily and welcomes people of all denominations.

DIRECTIONS AND INFORMATION

The Shrine of the Most Blessed Sacrament's address is 3224 County Road 548, Hanceville, Alabama 35077. County Road 548 runs off County Road 747, just south of Highway 91.

For information call (256) 352-6267 or visit their website www. olamshrine.com.

Resources

More Information

For more spiritual places and general information on spiritual traditions, the following is a list of valuable websites found on the World Wide Web. Although accurate at the time of publication, these sites can change or be discontinued at any time without notice.

SPIRITUAL PLACES

Franciscan Poor Clare Nuns of San Damiano Monastery: This is the website of the Franciscan Poor Clare Nuns of the San Damiano Monastery in Fort Myers Beach, Florida. It contains information about the monastery's history and activities. www.poorclares-fmb.org.

Hindu Society of Northeast Florida: This is an interesting website with information about the Hindu society in northeast Florida. www.jaxhindutemple.org.

Islamic Center of Northeast Florida: This website contains information about the Islamic center in northeast Florida, including activities, schedules, and news. www.icnef.org.

Monks of Adoration: This is an informative website of the Monks of Adoration, a small monastic community located in south Venice, Florida. www.monksofadoration.org.

Sisters of St. Joseph of St. Augustine: This is the website of the Sisters of St. Joseph of St. Augustine in Florida. The sisters are famous for their stained-glass artwork. www.ssjfl.com.

GENERAL REFERENCES

American Catholic: Maintained by Franciscan Friars, this website offers a variety of spiritual and practical information for Catholics. www.americancatholic.org.

Beliefnet: This website offers many articles, spiritual inspiration, links, and information about a diverse range of religious faiths. www.beliefnet. com.

Buddhist Information and Education Network: This is a website with international Buddhist references, articles, and links. www.buddhanet. net.

Catholic Online: This popular website contains a great deal of information about the Catholic faith. www.catholic.org.

Chabad: Maintained by the Chabad organization, this website covers a variety of topics and information for Jews worldwide. www.chabad.org.

Cistercian Order: This is the website of the Cistercian Order of the Strict Observance, also known as Trappist monks and nuns. Texts, events, and worldwide monastery information is provided on this site. www.ocso.org.

Cistercian Order USA: This website offers information and links to the Order of Cistercians of the Strict Observance (OCSO) monasteries in the United States. www.cistercian-usa.org.

Contemplative Outreach: This is the website of Contemplative Outreach, an international spiritual network that promotes Christian contemplation through the practice of Centering Prayer. Articles, references, and information about this method of meditation are offered on this site. www.centeringprayer.com.

Florida Jewish: This website contains a wealth of topics, references, and useful information for the Florida Jewish communities. www.floridajewish.com.

Insight Meditation Society: The Insight Meditation Society is a well-established nonprofit organization that offers Buddhist meditation retreats and instruction. The organization operates retreat facilities and a center for Buddhist studies. www.dharma.org.

Mastery Foundation: This is the website of the Mastery Foundation, an interfaith organization that works to empower people through dialogue and the practice of Centering Prayer. www.masteryfoundation.org.

Mount Athos: This is a unique website with information about Mount Athos in Greece. Mount Athos is home to twenty monasteries and is at the center of Eastern Orthodox monasticism. www.inathos.gr.

Order of Saint Benedict: This website offers information about the Benedictine Order, their monastic traditions and teachings. www.osb.org.

Orthodox Christian Information Center: This website has a variety of articles and information about the Orthodox Christian faith. www.orthodoxinfo.com.

Vipassana Meditation: This website contains information about Vipassana Meditation, including introduction, teachings, and practice. www.dhamma.org.

World Community for Christian Meditation: This is the website of the WCCM, a worldwide network of meditators that follow the contemplative practice of Christian meditation. The site includes many articles, references, teachings, as well as lists of meditation groups and retreats. www.wccm.org.

Bibliographic References

Bacovcin, Helen. *The Way of a Pilgrim.* New York, NY: Doubleday, 1992.

Barthel, Manfred. *The Jesuits.* New York, NY: William Morrow and Company, Inc., 1984.

Colliander, Tito. *Way of the Ascetics.* Crestwood, NY: St. Vladimir's Seminary Press, 2003.

Cummings, Charles. *Monastic Practices.* Kalamazoo, MI: Cistercian Publications, 1986.

Freeman, Laurence. *The Selfless Self.* New York, NY: The Continuum Publishing Company, 1998.

Fry, Timothy. *RB 1980: The Rule of St. Benedict in English.* Collegeville, MN: The Liturgical Press, 1982.

Renard, John. *The Handy Religion Answer Book.* Detroit, MI: Visible Ink Press, 2002.

Shimano, Eido. *Points of Departure.* Livingston Manor, NY: The Zen Studies Society Press, 1991.

Tvedten, Benet. *The View from a Monastery.* New York, NY: Riverhead Books, 1999.

Ware, Kallistos. *The Orthodox Way.* Crestwood, NY: St. Vladimir's Seminary Press, 2003.

Index

Paul of the Cross, Saint, 84–85
Paul, Saint, 23
Pennsylvania, 38, 51, 124
Peter, Saint, 23
Philadelphia, PA, 100
Philotheou Monastery, 17
Photios the Great, Saint, 22
Poland, 95
Poor Clares, 102, 127, 131
Presbyterian sites
    Memorial Presbyterian
      Church, 13–14, *13*
    Montgomery Conference
      Center, 15–16, *15*
Presbytery of St. Augustine, 15
Raja Gopuram, 94
Reddick, FL, 2–3, *2*
relics, 23
Rock Hill, SC, 120–21
Roman Catholic sites
    Ancient Spanish Monastery,
      68–70, *68, 69*
    Blessed Trinity Shrine
      Retreat, 100–101
    Campo San José, 71
    Cenacle Spiritual Life
      Center, 72–74, *73*
    Emmanuel Retreat House, 102–103
    Franciscan Center, 36–37, *36*
    Holy Name Monastery, 38–39, *38*
    Ignatius House Retreat
      Center, 112–114, *112, 113*
    Manresa Retreat House, 78–79, *78*
    Mary, Queen of the Universe
      Shrine, 44–46, *45*
    Marywood Retreat Center, 10–12, *11*
    Mepkin Abbey, 115–119, *117, 118*
    Monastery of the Holy Spirit,
      107–111, *107, 108*
    MorningStar Renewal
      Center, 80–81, *80*
    Mother of God House
      of Prayer, 82–83
    Oratory Center for
      Spirituality, 120–121

Our Lady of Divine
    Providence, 47–48, *47*
Our Lady of Florida Spiritual
    Center, 84-86, *84*
Our Lady of Mount Carmel
    Spiritual Life Center, 87–88
Our Lady of Perpetual Help
    Retreat Center, 89–90, *90*
Sacred Heart Monastery, 122–123
Saint Bernard Abbey, 124–125
Saint John Neumann
    Renewal Center, 21
Saint Leo Abbey, 39, 51–55, *52, 53*
Saint Mary Star of the Sea
    Spiritual Center, 91–92
San Pedro Center, 59–61, *59, 60*
Sea of Peace House of Prayer, 126
Shrine of Our Lady of La
    Leche, 25–28, *26, 27, 28*
Shrine of the Most Blessed
    Sacrament, 127–128
Rule of Saint Benedict, 38–39,
    51, 107, 110, 116, 122, 124
Russia, 95
Sacramenia, Spain, 68
Sacred Heart Monastery, 122–23
Safety Harbor, FL, 49–50, *50*
Saint Anthony Monastery, 17
Saint Bernard Abbey, 124–125
Saint Bernard de Clairvaux
    Episcopal Church, 69, *70*
Saint Bernard Preparatory School, 124
Saint John Renewal Center, 21
Saint Joseph Convent, 38
Saint Leo Abbey Golf Course, 53
Saint Leo Abbey, 39, 51–55, *52, 53*
Saint Leo University, 39, 51
Saint Mark's Cathedral, 13
Saint Mary Help Abbey, 51
Saint Mary Star of the Sea
    Spiritual Center, 91–92
Saint Nicholas Greek Orthodox
    Cathedral, 56–58, *57*
Saint Peter's Basilica, 125

About the Author

Mauricio Herreros has a bachelor's degree in computer science and an MBA. After fifteen years of working in the corporate world Mauricio felt a lack of purpose in his career. Five years ago he embarked on a personal journey that led him to discover the diverse and mostly unknown world of spirituality that exists all around us in Florida and the Southeast. This book is the result of that experience.

Lorrie Herreros

Mauricio lives in northeast Florida with his wife and children. When he is not traveling or writing, he works as a systems consultant. Spiritual Florida is his third book. He is also the author of *Running in Florida,* published by Pineapple Press.

If you liked *Spiritual Florida,* consider these titles from Pineapple Press:

Running in Florida by Mauricio Herreros. This complete guide presents detailed information on the 147 top places to run in Florida as well as on the 159 most remarkable and popular races. (pb)

Best Backroads of Florida by Douglas Waitley. Each volume in this series offers several well-planned day trips through some of Florida's least-known towns and little-traveled byways. You will glimpse a gentler Florida and learn lots about its history. Volume 1: The Heartland (south of Jacksonville to north of Tampa). Volume 2: Coasts, Glades, and Groves (South Florida). Volume 3: Beaches and Hills (North and Northwest Florida). (pb)

Florida's Finest Inns and Bed & Breakfasts by Bruce Hunt. From warm and cozy country bed & breakfasts to elegant and historic hotels, author Bruce Hunt has composed the definitive guide to Florida's most quaint, romantic, and often eclectic lodgings. With photos and charming pen-and-ink drawings by the author. (pb)

Guide to Florida Lighthouses (Second Edition) by Elinor De Wire. Its lighthouses are some of Florida's oldest and most historic structures, with diverse styles of architecture and daymark designs. (pb)

The Horses of Proud Spirit by Melanie Sue Bowles. The story of Proud Spirit Horse Sanctuary, where, with a heart as big as a pasture, author Melanie Bowles takes in listless and broken horses and gives them a loving home where they finally know safety. (hb)

A Land Remembered by Patrick Smith. This well-loved, best-selling novel tells the story of three generations of the MacIveys, a Florida family battling the hardships of the frontier, and how they rise from a dirt-poor cracker life to the wealth and standing of real estate tycoons. (Available in hb and pb. Also available in a student edition and a teacher's manual)

 PINEAPPLE PRESS • 941-739-2219 • WWW.PINEAPPLEPRESS.COM